Christine Ann Leatz is director of research for Instrument Makar, Inc., and is a PhD candidate in family and child ecology at Michigan State University, East Lansing.

unwinding

how to turn stress into positive energy

christine ann leatz

A SPECTRUM BOOK

prentice-hall, inc., englewood cliffs, new jersey 07632

Library of Congress Cataloging in Publication Data

Leatz, Christine Ann.
  Unwinding: how to turn stress into positive energy.

  (A Spectrum Book)
  Bibliography: p.
  Includes index.
  1. Stress (Psychology) 2. Success. I. Title.
BF575.S75L324   158'.1   81–10642
                 AACR2

ISBN 0-13-937888-X

ISBN 0-13-937870-7 {PBK.}

This Spectrum Book is available to businesses and organizations at a special discount when ordered in large quantities. For information, contact Prentice-Hall, Inc., General Book Marketing, Special Sales Division, Englewood Cliffs, N. J. 07632.

A SPECTRUM BOOK

10 9 8 7 6 5 4 3 2 1

Printed in the United States of America

Editorial production/supervision
  and interior design by *Heath Lynn Silberfeld*
Cover design by *Honi Werner*
Manufacturing buyer: *Cathie Lenard*

Prentice-Hall International, Inc., *London*
Prentice-Hall of Australia Pty. Limited, *Sydney*
Prentice-Hall of Canada, Ltd., *Toronto*
Prentice-Hall of India Private Limited, *New Delhi*
Prentice-Hall of Japan, Inc., *Tokyo*
Prentice-Hall of Southeast Asia Pte. Ltd., *Singapore*
Whitehall Books Limited, *Wellington, New Zealand*

contents

acknowledgments
ix

1
what this book is all about
1

warnings and cautions   3

2
check yourself out
6

coping behavior checklist   7
stress symptom checklist   10

life satisfaction checklist 12
life experiences checklist 18
personality type checklist 22

3
how stress works
30

the physiological side of stress 30
common stress patterns 35
common stress reactions 37
why people perceive stress differently 39

4
stress-related problems and disorders
45

psychosomatic illnesses 45
common stress-related problems 48
what doesn't work 73

5
anger, communication, and assertiveness
78

how anger works 78
how communication works 87
how assertiveness works 92

6
coping with the effects of stress
97

breathing exercises 99
visualization 100
behavioral rehearsal 104
self-massage 106

meditation   108
diet   110
physical fitness   120
favorite passions   123
guilty pleasures   124
rewards   124
journals and diaries   126
humor   127
hugs   128

7
values, goals, and decision making
130

values   130
setting goals   136
making wise decisions   138
what is your lifeline like?   140
taking risks   142
common decision-making mistakes   144

8
organizing your life and your time
148

why organize?   149
managing time   157
dealing with interruptions   161
ways to save time   163
managing procrastination   164
managing your money   166

9
the last word
171

10
good reads
173

how stress works   174
stress-related problems and disorders   174
anger, communication, and assertiveness   175
coping with the effects of stress   176
values, goals, and decision making   177
organizing your time and your life   178

index
179

acknowledgments

Writing this book while working sixty hours a week and going to school full time to complete my doctorate has been a very stressful experience! I learned a great deal about stress and came to value even more some very special people who helped me keep it together so that you can keep it together!

A *big* hug and my undying gratitude go to my parents, Don and Lily Leatz—especially to Ma, who was my first editor—for providing support, encouragement, and bucks during the last month so that I could write instead of hiring myself out as a temporary secretary when my jobs ran out before the writing and dissertation research did.

A pat, extra servings of tuna, and catnip mice go to Sam and Stuie, who kept me sane throughout the whole process.

Very special thanks and love go to Geraldine Hart, ACSW, without whom this book would not have been possible. She encouraged me to follow my own drummer and never failed to provide wise counsel, support, and unlimited knowledge when it was sorely needed.

Hugs and cheesecake go to my "second family"—Jan, Ellie, Gail, Gene, Bob, and Vicki—who kept up the good words, warm vibes, fun times, and hearty suppers when I really needed them.

Hugs and bottles of wine go to the "Human Ecology Contingent"—Pam, Margaret, Gail, Liz, Carrie, and Mari—who kept me laughing and provided superb role models of women balancing careers, education, and families while maintaining their sanity.

Warm thanks go to E. Jane Oyer, PhD, professor of family and child ecology at Michigan State University, whose encouragement, service as dissertation committee member extraordinaire, always available ear, and superb teaching skills enormously reduced my personal stress levels over the past several years.

Warm fuzzies go to all my special students at Lansing Community College and Michigan State University Evening College, who told me what they wanted to know about stress and taught me as much as I taught them.

Mucho appreciation goes to all the folks at Prentice-Hall's Spectrum Books, who took a chance on a two-page outline of an unsolicited manuscript idea and supported my efforts to produce the best book possible.

Finally, acknowledgment goes to Donna Manczak and the Michigan Cooperative Extension Service, whose actions provided the impetus for this book.

1

what this book is all about

Complete this sentence: I am _____.
If you are a typical "stress victim," you probably put "frazzled, worn-out, overworked and underpaid, too pooped to participate, worried, verging on the brink, a charter member of the Loony Tune Club, heading for the funny farm, bored, run-down," or a variety of expletives best left deleted!

You may have read a lot about stress and maybe even tried some suggested ways to relax. Most likely nothing really worked, and you find yourself asking why?

Why? Because you need to know about the *causes* of stress as well as ways to cope with the *effects* of stress. Causes of stress are our values, goals, priorities, decision-making skills, roles at home and on the job, communication abilities, and so forth—in short, all those known and unknown things that make us unique individuals. The effects of stress—anxiety, tension, headaches, fatigue, irritability, insomnia, and so on—are fairly common. But they are only *reflections* of those individual components that cause us to experience stress in the first place. I have found that stress will *not* go away until its causes are uncovered, dragged out into the open, and dealt with in some way. This is a tough job that requires guts—but unless you tackle it, all the relaxation techniques in the world aren't going to be worth a hill of beans.

This book will help you begin to explore your individual, unique causes of stress by helping you get to know yourself better through exercises and inventories. There are also lots of techniques, tricks, and tips included to help you cope with the *effects* of stress while you sort out the *causes*.

It's a holistic approach, one that involves the totality of your being, life-style, and environment. It's also fun! Besides, sometimes when life seems to be dealing you cards from the bottom of the deck, all you can do is shrug your shoulders, laugh, and say, "Aw, shoot!" (Or whatever!)

"Yeah, sure," I can just hear you thinking, "this sounds great, but how can I be sure this book will really work?" I cannot promise to completely erase stress from your life—the only time you will be completely free from stress is when you are dead—but I can tell you that this book has been carefully researched and then tested by hundreds of people, much like you, who found it very helpful.

How did this book get started? Several years ago, when I was working for the Michigan Cooperative Extension Service, I was assigned the task of developing a stress management program for families. This assignment caused me many sleepless nights and much stress, until I discovered an important fact. When I went back and reviewed the case histories of all the clients I had worked with as a social worker, I realized that every person had been seeking help for some problem that was an *effect* of stress. After further digging, I also found that there appeared to be five *causes* of stress: a person's values, his or her resources to cope with crises, a person's past experience with stressful situations, his or her feeling of control over the stressful situation, and each person's personality style.

As I did more research for the Cooperative Extension Service program, I learned a great deal about coping with the effects of stress, but found there was little information dealing with the causes of stress. You've probably discovered the same thing, and that may be why you picked up this book.

Using my training in social work, family therapy, and human ecology—along with personal experience gained from living a *very* stressful life—I developed a new way of looking at the causes of stress, one that involved values clarification, goal setting, decision-making skills, communication techniques, time and environment management, and problem-solving approaches.

I first tried these new ideas out in the Cooperative Extension Service program and then in classes on stress management I was teaching at Michigan State University and Lansing Community College. The people in these classes found the ideas to be very useful and applicable to their daily lives.

So the ideas in this book have been evaluated not only by physicians and mental health professionals but also by people like you, in situations similar to yours. It is a comprehensive program, and a comprehensive *anything* takes time. *This is not a crash or quickie stress reduction program!* The only way to get long-lasting results when working with a problem as complex as stress is to go slowly and thoroughly.

As you can see from the table of contents, this book covers everything from the physiological effects of stress to a list of "good reads"—good books you might want to look at for further information. Think of it as a smorgasbord waiting for you to approach it or as an adventure just about to begin. I guarantee that you will at least have some chuckles along the way!

But any program that involves your mind and body comes equipped with a set of warnings and cautions, and this book is no exception. So take heed.

warnings and cautions

1. *If you are under a physician's care for a stress-related illness or problem, get his or her permission before you try any of the suggestions given in this book.*

2. *Don't set overwhelming expectations for yourself.* Remember, Rome wasn't built in a day, and neither was the stressful situation(s) you presently find yourself in. It stands to reason that complex problems will take time to unravel, and while this book will help you with the unraveling process, it will not eliminate the need for it. So you're not doing anything wrong if you can't solve your problems overnight. (In fact, that's a good sign that you are doing something right!)

3. *Do a little at a time, not a lot all at once.* When you are under stress, you don't need the added stress of revamping your entire life all at once. Starting small eases the stress load, increases your confidence, and sets the stage for bigger things to follow.

4. *Not every suggestion works equally well for all people.* There is no single "magic" cure for stress. Because we are all so different and because the components of the causes of our stress are different, we may need different combinations of suggestions to help us reduce our stress levels effectively. Experiment with the suggestions offered in this book and develop a "package" of coping techniques that works best for you.

5. *Let the people around you know that you are beginning to make significant changes in your life.* Your friends and family are used to your old patterns of behavior and may be taken by surprise when you start reacting to them differently. To prevent any additional stress, put up a sign saying, "Please excuse any inconvenience you may experience. My life is currently under reconstruction. Thank you for your cooperation!"

6. *If you feel like you are getting in over your head at any time, be good to yourself and make an appointment to see a mental health professional to talk about it.* Everyone needs someone to talk to when the going gets rough, and mental health professionals make it their business to help people through those rough times.

Fair enough? At this point, at *least* two people in every stress management class or workshop I've ever run begin to panic! They get panicky because (a) they are afraid that when they find out what they are really like inside, they won't like what they find; or (b) they are afraid that they will have to do something "weird." Not to worry—on both counts. No one I have worked with ever found that they were terrible or awful inside, underneath it all. In fact, they all found out they were pretty darn terriffic! And nothing in this book is weird, strange, or far-out—I promise! If you feel uncomfortable about any inventory, exercise, or suggestion, don't do it! Do as much, or as little, as you are comfortable doing, *especially* if you are under a great deal of stress already.

Okay, sharpen those pencils, and let's get going!

2

check yourself out

In order to combat stress effectively, it is important to know the "enemy" inside and out. In other words, we need to clarify for ourselves exactly which areas of our lives are stressful and how we react to and cope with these situations. The following inventories are designed to help you accomplish just that.

Please read through the directions for each inventory and then respond *according to how you feel today*. If you feel uncomfortable with any question or inventory, don't answer it. However, the more inventories you respond to, the greater your self-knowledge about stress will be.

There are no right or wrong answers. The only "right" answers are those that are most true for *you*. So relax and have fun!

coping behavior checklist

The following checklist explores some common coping behaviors people can use when they find themselves in stressful situations. Please read through the following list and circle the responses that are true for you. Then add up your points and put your total score in the space provided at the end of the inventory.

0 Never used

1 Tried once

2 Used more than once in lifetime, but not monthly

3 Use 1-3 times per month

4 Use 1-2 times per week

5 Use 3 or more times per week

Coping Behavior

Physical exercise	0	1	2	3	4	5
Sleeping	0	1	2	3	4	5
Breathing exercises	0	1	2	3	4	5
Imagery training	0	1	2	3	4	5
Thought-stopping exercises	0	1	2	3	4	5
Behavioral rehearsal	0	1	2	3	4	5
Massage	0	1	2	3	4	5
Meditation or "centering"	0	1	2	3	4	5
Balanced diet	0	1	2	3	4	5
Hobby or hobbies	0	1	2	3	4	5
Talking to friends	0	1	2	3	4	5
Talking to family members, spouse	0	1	2	3	4	5
Crying	0	1	2	3	4	5
Shouting	0	1	2	3	4	5
Yoga or stretching exercises	0	1	2	3	4	5
Biofeedback	0	1	2	3	4	5

Deep muscle (or progressive) relaxation	0	1	2	3	4	5
Warm baths	0	1	2	3	4	5
Hugs (getting and giving)	0	1	2	3	4	5
Listening to music	0	1	2	3	4	5
Watching television	0	1	2	3	4	5
Going to a movie	0	1	2	3	4	5
Having sex	0	1	2	3	4	5
Reading "nonrequired" materials	0	1	2	3	4	5
Taking a vacation	0	1	2	3	4	5
Moderate drinking	0	1	2	3	4	5
Taking breaks	0	1	2	3	4	5
Taking naps	0	1	2	3	4	5
Giving yourself rewards	0	1	2	3	4	5
Organizing your living/ working space	0	1	2	3	4	5
Organizing homework/planning for research papers, term papers	0	1	2	3	4	5
Seeking professional help	0	1	2	3	4	5
Improving study skills	0	1	2	3	4	5
Taking classes to improve skills	0	1	2	3	4	5
Using community services	0	1	2	3	4	5
Taking classes to learn new activities	0	1	2	3	4	5
Dancing (any kind)	0	1	2	3	4	5
Window shopping or buying clothes	0	1	2	3	4	5
Attending plays, concerts, sports events	0	1	2	3	4	5
Doing arts/crafts activities	0	1	2	3	4	5
Scheduling/budgeting your time	0	1	2	3	4	5
Reordering priorities	0	1	2	3	4	5
Clarifying your values	0	1	2	3	4	5
Thinking about your goals	0	1	2	3	4	5
Practicing saying no	0	1	2	3	4	5
Taking a walk	0	1	2	3	4	5
Watching a sunset or sunrise	0	1	2	3	4	5
Playing a sport	0	1	2	3	4	5

Playing with/caring for a pet	0	1	2	3	4	5
Playing with your children	0	1	2	3	4	5
Going out with friends	0	1	2	3	4	5
Tending indoor/ outdoor plants	0	1	2	3	4	5
Other _____	0	1	2	3	4	5
Other _____	0	1	2	3	4	5
Other _____	0	1	2	3	4	5
Other _____	0	1	2	3	4	5
Other _____	0	1	2	3	4	5
Other _____	0	1	2	3	4	5
Other _____	0	1	2	3	4	5

*Coping Behavior Checklist Score*_____

what the coping behavior checklist shows

The higher your score on the Coping Behavior Checklist, the greater your chance for successfully coping with stress and preventing stress overload. Most people have tried several of these coping behaviors at one time or another, maybe without even knowing they *were* coping behaviors, so that a score of between 0 and 100 is fairly typical. If you scored between 100 and 150, you show a higher than average awareness of coping techniques. You can still stand to increase your practice of coping techniques, though, and you might want to consider experimenting with some of the coping techniques on the list that you haven't tried before. If you scored between 150 and 200, most likely you use a variety of coping techniques to get you through tough times, but you might not be aware that using coping techniques regularly has a *preventive* effect as well. Regular use of coping techniques can enhance recuperation times between crises and help your body function more effectively during crises. If you scored over 200, you are using a variety of coping techniques regularly to enhance your effectiveness in coping with stress. As our lives change, our needs for different coping techniques change as well. You might want to experiment with some new coping techniques from the list to increase your "bag of tricks" for future stressful situations.

stress symptom checklist

The following checklist explores some common reactions people experience when faced with stressful situations. Please read through the following list and circle the responses that are most true for you. Then add up your points and put your total score in the space provided at the end of the inventory.

0 Never experienced

1 Experienced once

2 Experienced more than once in lifetime, but not monthly

3 Experience 1-3 times per month

4 Experience 1-2 times per week

5 Experience 3 or more times per week

Reaction/Symptom

Pounding heart	0	1	2	3	4	5
Trembling/shaking	0	1	2	3	4	5
Teeth grinding	0	1	2	3	4	5
Insomnia (trouble falling asleep)	0	1	2	3	4	5
Frequent urination	0	1	2	3	4	5
Indigestion (upset stomach)	0	1	2	3	4	5
Stomach pain	0	1	2	3	4	5
Headache	0	1	2	3	4	5
Migraine headache	0	1	2	3	4	5
Fatigue	0	1	2	3	4	5
Constipation	0	1	2	3	4	5
Itching skin (dermatitis)	0	1	2	3	4	5
Acne	0	1	2	3	4	5
Blushing	0	1	2	3	4	5
Loss of appetite	0	1	2	3	4	5
Nightmares	0	1	2	3	4	5
Recurrent dreams	0	1	2	3	4	5
"Lump" in throat	0	1	2	3	4	5
Sore or tense neck muscles	0	1	2	3	4	5

Dry mouth	0	1	2	3	4	5
Sweaty palms	0	1	2	3	4	5
Excessive perspiration	0	1	2	3	4	5
Cold hands or feet	0	1	2	3	4	5
Low back pain	0	1	2	3	4	5
Hives	0	1	2	3	4	5
"Tight" or sore shoulders	0	1	2	3	4	5
Diarrhea	0	1	2	3	4	5
Troubled breathing	0	1	2	3	4	5
Tics	0	1	2	3	4	5
"Stuffy" sinuses	0	1	2	3	4	5
"Scratchy" or sore throat	0	1	2	3	4	5
Tendency to startle easily	0	1	2	3	4	5
Menstrual irregularity	0	1	2	3	4	5
Anxiety (feeling "uptight")	0	1	2	3	4	5
Increased desire to eat	0	1	2	3	4	5
Inability to respond sexually	0	1	2	3	4	5
Accident proneness	0	1	2	3	4	5
Eczema	0	1	2	3	4	5
Hair loss	0	1	2	3	4	5
Sore muscles in limbs	0	1	2	3	4	5
Waking up early and being unable to go back to sleep	0	1	2	3	4	5
Waking up often at night	0	1	2	3	4	5
Biting fingernails/ lips	0	1	2	3	4	5
Cold sores	0	1	2	3	4	5
Mental confusion	0	1	2	3	4	5
Absentmindedness	0	1	2	3	4	5
Inability to concentrate on a task	0	1	2	3	4	5
Crying	0	1	2	3	4	5
Feeling "blue" (depressed)	0	1	2	3	4	5
Considering suicide	0	1	2	3	4	5
Attempting suicide	0	1	2	3	4	5
Increased alcohol use	0	1	2	3	4	5
Increased drug use	0	1	2	3	4	5
Increased time spent sleeping	0	1	2	3	4	5
Other _____	0	1	2	3	4	5

		0	1	2	3	4	5
Other	_____	0	1	2	3	4	5
Other	_____	0	1	2	3	4	5
Other	_____	0	1	2	3	4	5
Other	_____	0	1	2	3	4	5
Other	_____	0	1	2	3	4	5

*Stress Symptom Checklist Score*_____

what the stress symptom checklist shows

The higher your score on the Stress Symptom Checklist, the greater the likelihood you are a victim of stress overload. Almost everyone has experienced several of these stress-related symptoms at some time during his or her life, so scores between 0 and 100 are normal. If you scored between 100 and 150, your body is telling you that you are in a high-stress situation, whether you are aware of it or not. If you scored between 150 and 225, you are most likely in a chronic stress situation, and the suggestions provided in this book will be very helpful for you. If you scored over 225 points, your chronic stress is very severe, and it might be a good idea for you to make an appointment for a checkup with your physician. He or she can help take care of your physical problems while you work on increasing your coping techniques by reading this book.

life satisfaction checklist

The following checklist will help you explore which areas in your life are currently stressful for you. Please answer the following sections according to how you feel today.

employment

Examples: My job is the pits.
I worry a lot about getting laid off.

Your thoughts: _____

_____

Overall are you:

_____ satisfied?

_____ dissatisfied?

school—education

Examples: I'm thinking about quitting school.
I'm thinking about going back to school.
I worry about taking tests.

Your thoughts: _____

_____

Overall are you:

_____ satisfied?

_____ dissatisfied?

friends

Examples: I have lots of good friends.
My best friend recently moved away.
I'd like to meet some new people.

Your thoughts: _____

_____

Overall are you:

_____ satisfied?

_____ dissatisfied?

family

Examples: I get lots of pressure about grades from home.

I enjoy visiting my family.
My parents are pressuring me to get married and
   settle down.
My kids drive me crazy sometimes.

Your thoughts: _____

_____

_____

Overall are you:

_____ satisfied?
_____ dissatisfied?

personal life

Examples: My boyfriend and I broke up recently.
   My spouse and I have been quarreling a lot.
   My lover and I have been getting along well.

Your thoughts: _____

_____

_____

Overall are you:

_____ satisfied?
_____ dissatisfied?

sex

Examples: It's hard for me to ask my lover for what I want.
   I really enjoy having sex with my lover.
   Sometimes I just don't feel like making love.

Your thoughts: _____

_____

_____

Overall are you:

_____ satisfied?
_____ dissatisfied?

energy

Examples: I'm tired much of the time.
I can always get geared up for fun things.
I'm really tired by Friday and look forward to the weekends.

Your thoughts: _____

_____

Overall are you:

_____ satisfied?
_____ dissatisfied?

health

Examples: Basically, I can't complain.
I get lots of headaches.
I'm worried about my health.

Your thoughts: _____

_____

Overall are you:

_____ satisfied?
_____ dissatisfied?

personal appearance

Examples: Some days I can't even stand to look in the mirror.
I'm definitely a "10."
I think I need some help in sharpening up how I look.

Your thoughts: _____

_____

Overall are you:

_____ satisfied?

_____ dissatisfied?

personal influence

Examples: I feel like a slave at work.

I look forward to going to work.

I get along well with other people.

Your thoughts: _____

_____

_____

Overall are you:

_____ satisfied?

_____ dissatisfied?

mood

Examples: I find my moods go up and down a great deal.

I worry about many things.

Some days I just feel blah.

Your thoughts: _____

_____

_____

Overall are you:

_____ satisfied?

_____ dissatisfied?

habits

Examples: I really should quit smoking.

I'm thinking about jogging again.

Basically I'm doing okay.

Your thoughts: _____

_____

_____

Overall are you:

_____ satisfied?

_____ dissatisfied?

living environment

Examples: I'm getting tired of hearing the neighbor's music through the walls of my apartment.

I think I've finally got my house just the way I want it.

I really like my condominium.

Your thoughts: _____

_____

_____

Overall are you:

_____ satisfied?

_____ dissatisfied?

leisure-time activities

Examples: I spend most of my free time watching TV.

I've been thinking about learning how to reupholster furniture.

I have lots of fun doing crossword puzzles.

Your thoughts: _____

_____

_____

Overall are you:

_____ satisfied?

_____ dissatisfied?

community involvement

Examples: I'm very active in programs with my church.
I vote, but that's about it.
Sometimes I think I spend too much time on all my volunteer activities.

Your thoughts: _____

_____

_____

Overall are you:

_____ satisfied?

_____ dissatisfied?

what the life satisfaction checklist shows

This checklist is geared to help you focus in on all the various parts of your life and then to think through whether you are satisfied with them as they are or whether you'd like parts of your life to change. The greater the number of areas in your life that you are happy with, the lower your potential for stress overload. If you are dissatisfied with any parts of your life, try to think why you might be dissatisfied. What obstacles are keeping you from having your life as you would like it to be? Can you think of ways around those obstacles? Think, too, about whether your expectations for changing your life are realistic. Too often we think that if we lost fifty pounds, became blond, and got a tan, people would think we were witty and intelligent, we'd make a million dollars, and our lives would suddenly be fantastic. In reality, that never happens. If we keep pushing for unrealistic goals, we only add needlessly to our stress levels. Are any of your expectations unrealistic?

life experiences checklist

Experts have found that there is a very strong correlation between the number of stressful experiences people experience during their lives and the state of their relative health or illness. Looking at recent experiences in our past often gives us a clue about vague feelings of stress that we may have, as well as helping us clarify values, goals, and priorities.

The following checklist is an adaptation of a *Life Experiences Inventory* developed by Dr. John Schneider, a professor in the Department of Psychiatry, College of Human Medicine, at Michigan State University. Dr. Schneider took the best aspects of a variety of life-experiences measures and developed a way for people to rate for themselves the impact the event had for them.

Look over the events in this checklist and decide if you have experienced any of them in the past year. Also include any events that may not have happened in the past year but that still affected you during that time, such as a divorce or death of a family member. Then rate the impact the experience had on your life: for example, a +3 rating would be an extremely positive impact, while a −3 would be an extremely negative impact.

When you have finished, total up the negative numbers and then total up the positive numbers you circled. Write both numbers in the spaces provided at the end of the checklist.

−3	Very negative
−2	Moderately negative
−1	Somewhat negative
0	No impact
+1	Somewhat positive
+2	Moderately positive
+3	Very positive

Life Experience

Marriage	−3	−2	−1	0	+1	+2	+3
Divorce	−3	−2	−1	0	+1	+2	+3
Separation	−3	−2	−1	0	+1	+2	+3
Reconciliation	−3	−2	−1	0	+1	+2	+3
Death of spouse	−3	−2	−1	0	+1	+2	+3
Death of close family member	−3	−2	−1	0	+1	+2	+3

Death of close friend	−3	−2	−1	0	+1	+2	+3
Sexual difficulties	−3	−2	−1	0	+1	+2	+3
Spouse starts work or school	−3	−2	−1	0	+1	+2	+3
Spouse stops work or school	−3	−2	−1	0	+1	+2	+3
Trouble with in-laws	−3	−2	−1	0	+1	+2	+3
Birth of child or adoption	−3	−2	−1	0	+1	+2	+3
Miscarriage or pregnancy	−3	−2	−1	0	+1	+2	+3
Child starts school or college	−3	−2	−1	0	+1	+2	+3
Child leaves home	−3	−2	−1	0	+1	+2	+3
Illness of family member	−3	−2	−1	0	+1	+2	+3
Loss of old friendship(s)	−3	−2	−1	0	+1	+2	+3
Formation of new friendship(s)	−3	−2	−1	0	+1	+2	+3
Illness/injury of close friend	−3	−2	−1	0	+1	+2	+3
Engagement	−3	−2	−1	0	+1	+2	+3
Breakup with boy/girlfriend	−3	−2	−1	0	+1	+2	+3
Reconciliation with boy/girlfriend	−3	−2	−1	0	+1	+2	+3
Change of residence	−3	−2	−1	0	+1	+2	+3
Change in social activities	−3	−2	−1	0	+1	+2	+3
Taking on mortgage over $15,000	−3	−2	−1	0	+1	+2	+3
Taking on mortgage under $15,000	−3	−2	−1	0	+1	+2	+3
Taking on loan of over $5,000	−3	−2	−1	0	+1	+2	+3
Taking on loan of under $5,000	−3	−2	−1	0	+1	+2	+3
Bankruptcy	−3	−2	−1	0	+1	+2	+3
Loss of job	−3	−2	−1	0	+1	+2	+3
Start of new job	−3	−2	−1	0	+1	+2	+3
Beginning of new school experience, for example, college or graduate school	−3	−2	−1	0	+1	+2	+3
New responsibilities on job	−3	−2	−1	0	+1	+2	+3
Salary increase	−3	−2	−1	0	+1	+2	+3
Salary decrease	−3	−2	−1	0	+1	+2	+3
Promotion	−3	−2	−1	0	+1	+2	+3
Outstanding personal achievement	−3	−2	−1	0	+1	+2	+3

Check Yourself Out

Start of major project at work/school	−3	−2	−1	0	+1	+2	+3
Completion of major project at work/school	−3	−2	−1	0	+1	+2	+3
Conflict on job/at school	−3	−2	−1	0	+1	+2	+3
Trouble with employer or instructor	−3	−2	−1	0	+1	+2	+3
Unemployment	−3	−2	−1	0	+1	+2	+3
On strike	−3	−2	−1	0	+1	+2	+3
Retirement or graduation	−3	−2	−1	0	+1	+2	+3
Christmas	−3	−2	−1	0	+1	+2	+3
Own birthday	−3	−2	−1	0	+1	+2	+3
Anniversary of significant event	−3	−2	−1	0	+1	+2	+3
Change in eating habits	−3	−2	−1	0	+1	+2	+3
Change in sleeping habits	−3	−2	−1	0	+1	+2	+3
Change in exercise patterns	−3	−2	−1	0	+1	+2	+3
Change in opportunities to relax	−3	−2	−1	0	+1	+2	+3
Major personal illness/injury	−3	−2	−1	0	+1	+2	+3
Chronic illness (personal)	−3	−2	−1	0	+1	+2	+3
Menopause or midlife crisis	−3	−2	−1	0	+1	+2	+3
Change in smoking habit	−3	−2	−1	0	+1	+2	+3
Change in alcohol/drug use	−3	−2	−1	0	+1	+2	+3
Loneliness	−3	−2	−1	0	+1	+2	+3

*Total Negative*_____

*Total Positive*_____

what the life experiences checklist shows

Research has shown that *both* positive and negative life experiences can produce stress reactions and symptoms. Most people experience more *severe* stress reactions and symptoms from negative life experiences, however. Therefore, you would ideally want to have a larger positive total than negative total. If your negative total was larger than your positive total, you might want to pay careful attention to coping techniques listed in this book. If you are experiencing stress symptoms, you might also want to consider checking them out with your physician.

Now disregard the positive and negative signs on your totals and add the two numbers together, giving you one large number. The higher this number is, the greater your chance for experiencing stress overload and resultant physical and mental symptoms. I've found that most people can tolerate a score here of between 0 and 50 points fairly well, hence this range is considered normal. If you scored between 50 and 100 points, you may be beginning to experience stress overload and its accompanying symptoms. The techniques and ideas in this book could help you prevent the stressful situations from becoming chronic. If you scored over 100 points, you are probably in a chronic stress situation. You will especially benefit from the techniques and exercises in this book. Plan to work with your physician to maintain your level of physical health, too.

personality type checklist

There seem to be three common personality types who differ in their approach to stressful situations. These types are referred to as A, B, and C for convenience' sake. This checklist will help you determine which personality type you are and give you some insight into how other personality types function in stressful situations.

Read through the following situations and then decide which of the available reactions would most resemble yours. After you have finished the checklist, add up the total number of *A*'s, *B*'s, and *C*'s you checked and write them in the spaces provided at the end of the checklist.

1. It's 4:45 P.M. on Friday, and you need cash for the upcoming weekend. You most likely would
    A. throw papers into your briefcase, break all traffic records to get across town to your bank, and curse loudly as the bank manager locked the door at 5 P.M.

B. clear off your desk and head for the bank, figuring that if you didn't make it in time, you'd borrow some cash from a family member or cash your paycheck at the grocery store.

C. finish work and take a leisurely trip to the bus stop. You did your banking at lunch.

2. You're sitting in a staff meeting (or history lecture) and not much is going on. You most likely would be

A. thinking about all the work piled up on your desk, planning your grocery list, wondering if you were getting any important calls, fuming because you really had better things to do, chewing on your fingernails, and hunting for antacid tablets.

B. daydreaming about a trip to the Bahamas.

C. writing a letter to your mother.

3. A friend is talking about life in New York City. You find yourself

A. interrupting him to talk about the latest in-spots for dining and dancing you read about in the *New York Times* on Sunday.

B. wondering why on earth anyone would enjoy living in such a huge, busy city.

C. listening carefully and filing away bits of information in case you ever get to go to New York.

4. You've been asked to address a group of representatives of various community groups. As you are giving your speech, you

A. use lots of gestures, change your tone of voice, and find yourself speeding up at the ends of sentences. You also notice some puzzled looks on the faces of some of the audience members.

B. find yourself slowing down and really enjoying the experience. You also notice a couple of people have fallen asleep.

C. keep the pace of your speech upbeat, throw in some jokes and sidelines, and even manage to use some artwork to illustrate your points. Afterward several of the members of the audience ask you to speak for their group, too.

5. You and your friends are sitting around on a warm Saturday evening, drinking a few beers, and shooting the breeze. You find yourself

A. talking about things that are of interest to you. When somebody tries to change the subject, you find it impossible *not* to throw in your two cents' worth.

B. mostly listening to what everybody else is doing. You feel pretty good just drinking beer and enjoying being with your friends.

C. listening carefully to conversations and throwing in a little levity when things start to get too serious or heated. After all, it's Saturday night, and it's time for fun, not heavy discussion! You do your bit to keep the conversation lively and interesting, even playing the devil's advocate on occasion.

6. You teach at a school in a rural area, and when you turned on the radio this morning, you learned that because of the ice storm last night, classes have been cancelled. You most likely would

A. put on your boots, warm up the car, and head into school anyway, thinking that it would be an excellent time to catch up on all those papers that need to be graded.

B. turn off the radio, unplug the coffeepot, and go back to bed.

C. fix yourself a fancy breakfast, spend time doing the crossword puzzle in the newspaper, and start on the new bestseller from your book club.

7. You're having lunch with your best friend, and he asks if you notice anything different about him. You most likely would

A. be taken aback. You can't see anything different and don't know what to say. You mumble something about not being too observant these days, and your friend chuckles knowingly.

B. compliment him or her on the ten-pound weight loss. You knew right away that he or she must have *really* lost some weight! You tell your friend he or she looks fantastic and decide to skip dessert.

C. comment on the fact that your friend looks positively glowing and healthy, asking what his or her secret was for looking so great when everyone else is falling apart. You know your friend looks different, but you're not exactly sure why. You *hope* it's because he or she's been taking better care of him or herself.

8. When you picked up this book from the bookrack in the store, you were particularly interested in the chapter on organizing your time and your life. You hope it will

A. help you do more in less time, so that you can fit more things into your day.

B. give you a few tips on how to *look* organized, even if you really aren't. That way maybe your family will quit nagging you about being so slow.

C. give you some ideas on shortcuts so that you can spend more time doing needlepoint and playing with your kids.

9. Your spouse asks you what you did at work today. You say

A. "I sold four new accounts and increased the purchase orders from five of my old accounts. I think I managed to get two or three possible accounts lined up for tomorrow."

B. "Well, a little of this and a little of that. Not as much as I had hoped, but enough to get by."

C. "The best part of the day was track practice afterward. This is the first time I've been a coach, and I just *loved* watching the kids learn to respect their bodies and feel good about what they accomplished!"

10. A genie in a magic bottle says she'll grant you three wishes. You wish for

A. presidency of the company, membership in the country club, and one hundred more wishes.

B. long, happy lives for you and your family, a chance to be a better person, and maybe a dishwasher, if it wouldn't be too much trouble.

C. Besides world peace, you really can't think of anything you *really* want so much that you couldn't live without it.

11. On the tennis court you

A. become a real tiger. Your killer instinct functions at top form and you *want to win!*

B. like to be sociable and have a good time. You like it best when no one keeps score and you head for the club house afterward for a cool drink.

C. shake your head when your partner keeps insisting you rush the net and score points. The only thing you *hate* about tennis is the competition part. It takes all the fun out of it. Personally you just like to run around in the sun and swing at tennis balls. You know you will never be champion material, but somehow you really don't care.

12. It's Saturday morning, and you are standing in the checkout line at the neighborhood grocery store. Most likely you would be

A. trying to figure out if any other line would be shorter, thinking about all the other things you want to get done before noon, and mentally concentrating on throwing daggers at the woman ahead of you, who just decided to try and cash a check without three pieces of ID.

B. reading *People* magazine and maybe even *National Enquirer,* if you felt wicked enough. You might also be watching the other people and wondering how that woman in the next line could possibly feed all her children without going broke.

C. munching on cookies from the bag you just bought, contemplating the fact that you can learn a lot about people by what they have in their grocery carts, and trying to picture what kind of life the man ahead of you in line must have with caviar and diapers in his cart.

13. Your ten-year high school reunion is coming up. Most likely you would

   A. spend hours trying to find the outfit that would announce you have "arrived." You also try to think of clever conversational gambits that allow you to sneak in the fact that you now have a doctorate in Far Eastern languages, the UN wants you to do secret work for them, and you just sold your condo for $100,000 profit.

   B. look forward to seeing some of your old friends and sharing baby pictures with them. You also get a little excited thinking about seeing your old flame after all these years.

   C. Not go. You feel uncomfortable at those things anyway and feel people put up a false front just to make everyone else feel lousy. You decide to have a get-together for a couple of your best high school friends and their families a couple weeks after the reunion. That way the pressure will be off, and you all can relax and have fun.

14. You took up painting as a hobby several years ago, and when a professional artist noticed one of your paintings in your living room, he said that it was very definitely salable. He even knew of an art dealer who might be interested. You

   A. immediately started figuring out how much you could ask for it and how much the other ones in your attic could bring in.

   B. blushed, hemmed and hawed, and told the artist he was just being nice. Besides, his pictures were *really* pretty.

   C. thanked him for the compliment but declined the offer, mainly because you prefer to paint for fun. Thinking of selling a painting while you were creating it would take all the fun out of the experience for you.

*Total A's*_____

*Total B's*_____

*Total C's*_____

what the personality type checklist shows

Each of the situations mentioned in the checklist represents situations that the three stress-personality types would handle very differently. The letter for which you had the highest total indicates the personality type you most resemble. Few people are "pure types" (meaning that all their answers were for one personality type); most people are a mix of all three personality types. However, you may tend to resemble the personality type for which you had the highest total.

IF YOU HAD MORE As   Type A people are usually hardworking, striving, competitive people. They try to do a lot in very little time and often feel rushed because they don't plan for the unexpected in their overcrowded schedules. Research has shown that Type A people have a much higher risk of cardiovascular disease, heart attacks, and strokes than either Type B or Type C. If you resemble a Type A, you will want to study the techniques and exercises presented in this book carefully—they might save your life!

IF YOU HAD MORE Bs   Type B people are typically more "laid-back" than Type A's. They don't feel compelled to prove how great they are and are content to enjoy life as it comes. If you resemble a Type B, you might want to study the ideas presented in this book to help you cope with Type A's! Type B's most frequently experience stress symptoms when Type A's expect them to behave like A's. Be good to yourself if you're in that kind of situation. The exercises and techniques presented in this book have a preventive effect, too and can help you prepare for a world full of A's.

IF YOU HAD MORE Cs   Type C people are somewhat rare, mainly because it takes a high level of maturity and self-acceptance to be a Type C. Type C people are more concerned about the process of tasks and events rather than their outcomes and measure their successes and failures differently than either Type B or Type A. Of all the personality types, Type C's have the least chance of exhibiting stress symptoms and problems, mainly because their psychological mind set toward life is very accepting and philosophical. They also know they will fail sometimes, so they don't worry about it. On the outside Type C's may *look* like Type A's. Type C's are very active, are often involved in many projects and groups, have lots of energy, and accomplish great things. They work hard, but they also like to play and relax. I'd like *everyone* to become a Type C, mainly because a Type C usually enjoys his or her work so much that it has become play. These people truly *enjoy* what they are doing, and sometimes even feel guilty about being paid for having so much fun! I've found that a B can easily become a C, and many seem to do so naturally as they get older, but it can be difficult for an A to become a C. Type A's *can* effect behavior changes, however, and who knows, with all the drive Type A's have, they just might make it to C if they really want to!

3

how stress works

In order to combat stress effectively, it is essential to know the "enemy" inside and out. If you know how stress affects your mind and body, you will be able to determine how to short-circuit the process. And that's what this chapter is all about.

the physiological side of stress

The "grandfather" of human stress research is Hans Selye, who first documented some of the physiological aspects of stress in the 1930s. What he found out then still holds true today.

Selye discovered that there are two kinds of stress. The first kind, which he called "acute stress," occurs when there is an immediate threat to a person's life or physical being, and the person has to respond instantaneously. A good example is going into a skid on an icy road while driving your car. You have to be able to react fast, and if you've ever been in a similar situation, you probably noticed that your hands shook, your heart raced, and maybe your knees felt a little weak afterward. That reaction happened as a result of adrenaline and noradrenaline, two biochemicals produced by your body to decrease your reaction time and sharpen your senses. Adrenaline and noradrenaline produce a "rush," leaving you feeling a little drained when it's over. Adrenaline has helped people do miraculous things in a crisis. It has enabled people to lift cars off injured people and to accomplish many other extraordinary things.

A second kind of stress is one Selye called "chronic stress," and that is the kind most people reading this book are probably familiar with. Chronic stress occurs when a crisis situation is prolonged without any rest or recuperation time for your body. Most of the stressful situations people experience today are a result of their roles at home and on the job, which produce chronic stress situations.

Unfortunately, chronic stress situations trigger the production of different biochemicals in our bodies. The adrenal cortex, a small organ at the base of the brain, produces biochemicals called corticoids in an effort to help your body respond to a stress situation, and corticoids are the "bad guys." While adrenaline and noradrenaline are easily broken down by your body, and any excess can be flushed out of your system through your kidneys, corticoids are too large structurally to be eliminated the same way. Unless they are biochemically altered in some way, corticoids remain in your system, where they are capable of raising your blood pressure, damaging your kidneys, increasing the likelihood of cardiovascular disease by facilitating the adhering of fats in arteries and veins, and a whole host of other problems. Corticoids are also capable of actual physical tissue damage. Chronic stress also increases the amounts of hydrochloric acid present in your stomach and upper gastrointestinal system. That's why you get heartburn and stomach pain when you are under stress.

What triggers acute and chronic stress situations? Researchers have found that *any* situation can be perceived by a person as stressful, given the right conditions. Selye found that *both* chronic and acute stresses produce a definite series of reactions in the human body, which he called the General Adaptation Syndrome (GAS). This syndrome works as follows.

The first phase is the *alarm* phase and occurs when your brain and body perceive some sort of threat to you in the environment or a situation that requires your immediate attention. Adrenaline and noradrenaline are rapidly produced and rushed throughout your body to prepare you for action.

The second phase is the *resistance* phase, which occurs when your body readies a particular organ or muscle group to cope with and resolve the stressful situation. Most of the time your body chooses the organ group most suited to handle the crisis situation, for example, your leg muscles if you need to run, your arm muscles if you need to strike out at somthing, and so on. If it is not safe for you to do anything about the situation, such as when you have a quarrel with a co-worker or with your spouse, your body may shift the coping responsibility to your heart or stomach.

The second phase is crucial for coping with the effects of the stressful situation and preventing tissue damage. If you are able to act in some way to use up the adrenaline and noradrenaline, resolving the situation so that no threat to your well-being remains, GAS ends here. You have either "fought or fled" the stressful situation. But—and this is a big but—if you are not able to impact upon the situation to alleviate the crisis, your body responds to the situation as a chronic stress situation, and corticoids begin to be formed.

Something else crucial happens at this time as well. Remember that your body shifted the coping responsibility to an organ or muscle group in your body during the first part of the resistance phase. Any organ group can only last for a given amount of time before it becomes exhausted and can no longer cope with the stress situation effectively. How long and how well any particular organ or muscle group will cope depends upon the following.

1. *Your heredity.* Heredity affects your ability to cope with stress because, to some extent, your family genes can play a role in the overall wellness of a particular organ or muscle group. Some families have a predisposition to heart disease, others to stomach problems, and so on.

2. *Your overall level of health.* The healthier you are to begin with, the longer it will take the corticoids to have an impact strong enough to exhaust the particular organ or muscle group.

3. *Your environment.* Environment can be a significant contributing factor to how well you are able to stand up to stress. It can either add to the damage going on or increase your overall level of wellness. For example, consider the following situation: Ann's family has a predisposition to stomach ulcers, and lately she has been having problems with heartburn and upset stomach. This morning she covered a very important news story for her paper that took longer than she had anticipated. It is 2 P.M., and she is on deadline. She can only grab a quick lunch on the run, and the closest spot for that is a taco stand. Ann chooses a couple of spicy burritos and washes them down with strong coffee. Her editor reads her story over her shoulder while she types out the copy on her video-readout terminal. When the paper finally gets to bed, Ann notices that she has a whale of a stomach ache and starts looking around for her antacid tablets. Chances are that Ann's stomach isn't going to last long at this rate!

4. *The severity of the stressful situation.* The more severe the stressful situation, the higher your corticoid output. With lower levels of stress, your corticoid level is lower, which gives your body a chance to alter the corticoids biochemically, making them structurally smaller so that they can be removed from your bloodstream through your kidneys.

5. *Your energy level.* Everyone has an optimal amount of energy they can command at any one time. This optimal level of energy is determined by your health, daily nutrition, upbringing, and personality. When more than one worry or crisis is occurring at the same time, your energy has to be diverted to handle each of the crisis situa-

tions. This means that you have less energy available to handle each individual crisis. The less energy you can supply to an organ or muscle group, the faster it will become exhausted.

Eventually your "first-choice organ group" will become exhausted and damaged. If the stressful situation is still present, your body will switch the coping responsibility to another organ or muscle group. That's why some people get a skin rash after they get asthma or develop low back pain after they get an ulcer. If the stressful situation is *still* not resolved, eventually the second organ or muscle group will become exhausted, and your body will shift the coping responsibility to a third organ group, and on and on.

If the stressful situation has not been resolved by the time you have come to the end of your "organ chain"—or your rope, so to speak—your body will reach what Selye calls the exhaustion phase. This phase results in severe illness or death. You've used up all your reserves and resources, and your body can no longer handle the stressful situation for you.

It usually takes a long time to reach the exhaustion phase. But if for some reason your body picks your weakest organ or muscle group to handle the stress first, you may reach your personal exhaustion point much faster than someone else.

There are ways to short-circuit GAS. One way is to act in some way to resolve the stressful situation during the alarm phase, thus preventing corticoid formation. A second way is to get some form of physical exercise when you are in the resistance phase. Researchers have found that physical activity and the biochemicals your body produces during such activity can structurally alter the corticoids so that they are less harmful and can be flushed from the bloodstream. A third way is to allow adequate resting time for your body between stressful situations. Your body is capable of repairing initial tissue damage done by corticoids if given enough recuperation time. Recuperation time can be shortened if you practice some sort of stress-reducing or relaxation technique during resting times. Later chapters in this book will help you determine which techniques could be most useful for you.

common stress patterns

What kind of stress patterns do people commonly have? Optimally your stress pattern should look like the first one shown in the figure. This stress pattern allows adequate rest and recuperation time between crises. How much time needed for rest and recuperation depends upon the severity of tissue damage and your overall level of health. Thus everyone will have a different optimal resting time.

But most people have stress patterns similar to the second one shown in Figure 1. There is less than adequate resting time between crises. However, you can *enhance* your body's recuperative powers by practicing coping and relaxation techniques and including wellness behaviors in your daily life. If you take care of yourself, it is possible to survive even a severe stressful situation with minimal damage to your body.

The third stress pattern pictured in Figure 1 is considered harmful. This drawing represents a chronically stressful situation that begins and doesn't let up. High levels of corticoid production occur in this situation, which can cause actual tissue damage. However, your body can learn to adapt to high levels of stress biochemicals and function adequately in such situations, as long as is needed to preserve your survival. Problems occur *after* the stressful situation has ended. Very often people who have survived such stress patterns develop delayed stress reactions, ranging from mental problems to heart disease and death. Many soliders who fought in the Vietnam War developed delayed stress reactions several years *after* they had returned to their families in the United States, causing nightmares, personality changes, violent behavior, and chronic physical problems.

The fourth stress pattern pictured in Figure 1 is the one researchers consider to be the most dangerous. This pattern is made up of a series of crises coming rapidly one right after the other, with very little resting time between each crisis. The tiny resting period is enough to allow your body to quit producing corticoids and to begin reestablishing new equilibriums of body biochemicals, when suddenly it has to gear up to cope with a new crisis all over again. This type of

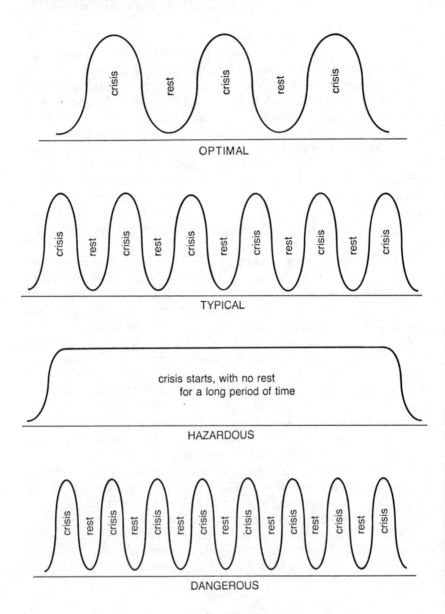

Figure 1. *COMMON STRESS PATTERNS*

"yo-yo" syndrome is *extremely* hard on your body, and people experiencing this type of stress pattern reach the exhaustion phase faster than people experiencing other stress patterns.

common stress reactions

When people find themselves in stressful situations, how do they respond? The most effective reaction is to find some way to deal with the situation actively and resolve the crisis it has caused. But sometimes we cannot do that.

As a therapist, and oftentimes stressed human being, I've found that people usually react in one of seven ways to a stressful situation.

1. The first response most people experience is *tolerance*. You just put up with the situation and go on as best you can.

2. After a while, though, tolerating the situation isn't enough. Most people next try *diversion*. Diversion involves doing anything that takes your mind off the situation for a while and gives you a much-needed mental or physical break. Common diversions are going to the movies, watching TV, reading books and magazines, playing sports, working on hobbies, fighting, eating, making love, meditating, and so forth. You're not working directly on the problem to resolve it, but you are doing something to expend some of the energy and frustration you may be feeling.

3. If the stressful situation still hasn't been resolved, some people begin to practice *withdrawal*. Withdrawal means removing yourself physically or mentally from the stressful situation. Common withdrawal responses range from unplugging the telephone, oversleeping, running away, or getting drunk to more serious withdrawal techniques, such as suicide, drug abuse, or deep depression.

4. If withdrawal doesn't work, many people practice *denial*. In

effect, they deny to themselves, and often to others around them, that there is a stressful situation at all. They try to fool themselves by pretending that things are just as they were before the stressful situation began. Denial usually makes the stressful situation worse and adds to the toll already taken on the body.

5. Another response some people choose in extremely stressful situations is *"going crazy."* Sometimes going crazy is a very sane thing to do. It is a last-ditch attempt at self-survival in an overwhelming situation. Long-term "craziness" is not especially beneficial to most people in the long run, but it can provide a breathing space and make an intolerable situation bearable for a little while. It might also keep a person alive.

6. If toleration, diversion, withdrawal, and denial haven't worked, people often respond by developing some sort of *illness*. The corticoids produced as a result of this chronic stress situation have done actual tissue damage, making the person ill. Physicians often call these illnesses "psychosomatic," and we usually think that means that our aches and pains are all in our head. Not so! The corticoids our bodies are producing do damage tissue and wear down our reserves of energy, making us more susceptible to a wide range of illnesses.

7. If all the previously mentioned responses haven't worked to alleviate the stressful situation, *death* can result. Death is the ultimate coping technique. It is also the end result of GAS and biochemical damage. Most people are lucky enough never to reach this final stress point, and the purpose of this book is to make sure you never do, either.

None of these common responses to stress—toleration, diversion, withdrawal, denial, going crazy, illness, or death—is an effective way to cope with stress. The only really effective way to deal with stressful situations is to resolve them. But it is important to respect these other common reactions for what they are—valiant attempts to survive in overwhelming situations. They are not "bad" or "wrong," they just are.

why people perceive stress differently

What makes one person respond with withdrawal while another person responds by actively confronting a stressful situation? I've found that the answer to that question lies in how people perceive stressful events. And our perceptions are based upon our values, resources, track record, feelings of control, and personality style.

values

Your values play a big part in your perception of a situation as stressful because they determine the meaning the situation has for you. It stands to reason that you will be more upset, henced stressed, if something goes wrong with something you care a great deal about than you will be if something goes wrong with a situation you don't care that much about.

For example, Kay had always felt that how she (and her apartment) looked was very important. She spent a large portion of her salary on clothes and furnishings and really enjoyed receiving compliments on both. Kay saw herself as the trend setter in her group of friends and prided herself on being able to spot trends before anyone else did. When she was laid off of her job, it came as a real shock. Most of Kay's salary had gone for purchases, and she had little saved. Unable to continue her purchasing of new clothes and furnishings, Kay felt her self-esteem dwindling. Not being able to buy new clothes bothered her a great deal, and when she had to sell some of her furniture, she was devastated.

Kay put a high value on "looking good," and when her life situation changed and she couldn't look as "good" as she wanted to, a severe stress situation resulted.

resources

The amounts and kinds of resources you have available to use in coping with a crisis can determine how stressful the crisis will be for you. People usually think "resources" refer to money, education, job skills, or savings. But resources are much more than that. Resources are anything that helps you cope more effectively with a crisis situation. Resources can include family, friends, physical health, availability of information, knowledge of relaxation techniques, communication skills, organizational ability—in short, your "bag of tricks." If you can increase the number and kind of resources in your bag of tricks, you can greatly increase your ability to cope with stressful situations effectively.

track record

Your track record is built upon your past experiences with stressful situations. If you have handled crisis situations to your satisfaction in the past, chances are you feel good about yourself. If you feel good about yourself and your abilities, you're more likely to believe that there is *something* you can do about a crisis, and you will at least begin to find some ways to cope. But if your past experiences with handling crisis situations have been negative, you might give up in a new crisis situation without even trying. In addition, if you have handled stressful situations effectively in the past, you learned a wide variety of problem-solving skills you may not even be aware you know.

feeling of control

If you believe you can control the *outcome* of a situation in any way, you will feel less threatened by that situation and may be able to tolerate higher levels of stress that result. It's situations that people feel they have no control over that are stressful and frustrating.

In addition, I've found that we often have more control in situations than we think we have. Even if we cannot control the outcome of a situation (such as in divorce), we may be able to have some sort of impact on the *process* leading to the outcome (such as arranging adequate child support, clarifying visitation rights, dividing property, and so on). If that fails, we are *always* capable of changing our *perception* of the situation itself (for example, "I'm not losing a marriage, I'm gaining a chance to grow and develop as a person").

personality style

There seem to be three different kinds of people when it comes to stressful situations. One type of person tends to see everything as a crisis. This person is usually hardworking, goal-oriented, compulsive, and lives a highly structured life. Some researchers have named this type of person Type A. Another kind of person is a little more easygoing, slow moving, and less outcome-oriented. He or she sees some situations as crises, and researchers call this kind of person Type B. A third personality type really doesn't view much of anything as a crisis. Such people are more concerned with the process of life and not its outcomes; they have lots of energy, feel competent, and depend on themselves to set goals for their life. I call this type of person Type C. Type C people seem to suffer from stress reactions less frequently than either Type A or Type B. Type A people have been found to suffer a higher incidence of cardiovascular disease, heart attacks, and strokes than either Type B or Type C. Type B's most often experience stress reactions when they are placed in situations where they are expected to perform in a Type A manner. This is extremely stressful for B's and "going against type" for B's often leads to physical stress reaction symptoms.

how perception works

It is my theory that people perceive situations as stressful based upon their values, resources, track record, feelings of control, and personality style. You can *change* your perception of a stressful situation by changing any one, or any combination of, these five components of perception.

Since our modern life-styles are often collections of habits, clarifying our values for ourselves is very important. It's important to find out not only what our values are but also whether these values are currently useful for enhancing our life-styles. Values we may have acquired as children (such as roles for adults to play in the world) may no longer be useful, given the massive changes our society has gone through in the recent past. Holding on to values that aren't helping us get on with our lives is stress producing. But it is possible to sort through our values, toss out those that are no longer useful, and keep those that are life enhancing. Later chapters in this book will help you do just that.

Developing your "bag of tricks" by increasing the resources you have at your command for coping with stress is probably the easiest component to work on. That's what this whole book is about! Every new skill and technique you learn will add to your ability to cope—even if you don't pull it out of your bag of tricks until several years from now. It's an immensely reassuring feeling to be sitting on a bulging bag of tricks!

Improving and building upon your track record is a little harder to do, but it be done. Each new situation you handle to your satisfaction, no matter how small, increases your track record—and the effect is cumulative. It's also helpful to focus more clearly on your successes than to keep all your attention on your failures. If you're like me, you know every single one of your failures in great detail, but when asked to talk about what you do well, you're at a loss for words. Give yourself a pat on the back when you "do good." It's *not* bragging or blowing your own horn—it's called being realistic!

It is possible to reclaim control for your own life and the situations you find yourself in. Repeat after me three times: "I am in charge of myself, my feelings, and my actions. No one has control over me unless I give him or her that control." And whatever you've given away, you can take back.

Of all the components of perception, your personality style is probably the most difficult to change. Even if you can't change your personality style, you can get to know it better and build in allowances for it when you are in crisis situations.

Let's look at a simple example and see how the perception and coping processes work.

Not too long ago I lost my job at a child abuse prevention agency when federal and state funding monies were cut back due to a recession.

Assume for a minute that I need 100 points overall for my Perception Quotient in order to cope effectively with a crisis situation.

Values: I rated myself −60 points because I had very strong feelings about having a job, being able to eat, and keeping a roof over my head. I was also finishing my doctorate and highly valued being able to pay for the tuition that involved. (Strong values are rated negatively because when these values are upset in some way, you get upset!)

Resources: I rated myself +50 points because I had a variety of salable job skills, knew where to look for new jobs, had a large circle of supportive friends, knew I could count on my family to back me up, and was familiar with a wide range of stress-reducing relaxation techniques.

Track Record: I rated my track record +50 points also. I had experienced similar situations in the past and had handled them effectively. I had been able to find new jobs in the past and adjust to them successfully.

Feeling of Control: I rated my feelings of control at −10 points, because the loss of the job wasn't my fault and because nothing I could do would create funds to keep me employed at the agency.

Personality Style: I'm a Type C, so I scored +30 points. Type B score +20 points, and Type A people score +10 points.

After adding up my scores, I came up with 60 points overall, still well below the 100 needed to cope effectively with the situation. What to do?

I decided I didn't want to change my values in this area, couldn't change my track record, and didn't want to change my personality style. But I could increase my resources and feelings of control. So I increased my resources by +10 points, bringing my new resources total to +60 points. I did that by rewriting my résumé, getting acquainted with new people in my field, tracking down job leads, and learning new skills in graphics and audiovisual development.

But most importantly, I added +30 points to my feelings of control by creating a course on stress management and offering to teach it at two universities and by opening my own "corner of the kitchen table" business—I started a consultation practice doing seminars and workshops on stress management for business and community groups. That brought my new control score up to +20 points.

The total of my new Perception Quotient turned out to be 100 points, the amount necessary to cope effectively with the stressful situation, and I was able to weather the storm and keep a roof over my head! As a result the crisis was uncomfortable and somewhat stressful, but it was not devastating. Most importantly, it did not turn into a chronic stress situation.

This whole process was not that difficult to accomplish. You are fully capable of doing the same thing. The rest of this book will show you how!

4

stress-related problems and disorders

psychosomatic illnesses

Stress-related problems and disorders are often called psychosomatic (from the words *psyche,* meaning mind, and *soma,* meaning body). Many people think that means the problem is "all in your head" and will go away if you "just relax and stop worrying about it." This myth is a result of psychoanalytic theory that was developed *before* researchers discovered that stress biochemicals could actually cause physical tissue damage and trigger many health problems.

The old psychoanalytic theory of psychosomatic illness went like this: A person finds himself or herself in a situation that is hard to resolve. As the situation becomes more overwhelming, he or she begins to fear there is no way out. At that point he or she makes an unconscious choice to become ill as a way of coping with an intolerable situation.

Because of this old unproven theory, psychosomatic illnesses began to acquire a very negative connotation. You were somehow weak or lacking in willpower if you developed a psychosomatic illness. And physicians began to label every problem they couldn't adequately diagnose as psychosomatic.

a new approach

Bunk! I feel it is time for a new definition of psychosomatic illness. I have worked as a therapist with people suffering from a variety of psychosomatic illnesses, and believe me, often it wasn't all in their head. Sometimes it was in their stomach or lungs!

That old psychoanalytic theory of psychosomatic illnesses may be true for some people, but most of the time it is not. Research is beginning to document new kinds of psychosomatic illnesses— illnesses that are the result of prolonged impact on the General Adaptation Syndrome on the human body.

Because of the complex biochemical changes, depletion of energy reserves, and corticoid production it causes, the General Adaptation Syndrome (GAS) can cause actual tissue damage over a prolonged period of time. GAS can increase the amount of acid secreted in the stomach, leading to gastritis and ulcers; disrupt normal flora in the intestinal tract, causing diarrhea; constrict blood vessels, leading to headaches and high blood pressure; and on and on—the list is growing almost every day.

Consequently, *these illnesses are not unconsciously chosen.* They are the result of wear and tear on the body caused by GAS. What does this mean? Too often people classify such problems as "mind-induced" and go no further with them. But it is important for those suffering from them to make sure they are not physically based.

checking it out

If you are experiencing any physical symptoms that seem to be related to stress, it is a good idea to visit your family physician and get those symptoms checked out. Hopefully you have a family physician you feel comfortable with and trust. Your physician will probably take a careful history of your symptoms and give you a thorough examination. Laboratory tests and X rays may be used, but not everyone needs them. If no evidence of serious organic illness is found, changes in your diet, daily activities, or possibly medication may be used to help bring your problem under control.

partners in the battle

One of the most important parts of good medical care is your physician's "bedside manner." Reassurance, comfort, and open communication are as important for a physician to provide as superb diagnostic skills and surgical know-how. Good communication between physician and patient is a two-way street, and you have an equal responsibility for maintaining and improving that communication process.

1. *Don't be afraid to ask questions.* (Even if it looks like your physician is ready to fly out of the door of the examining room!) You have probably paid a considerable amount of money to see your physician, and you are entitled to getting your money's worth. And that includes getting your questions answered.

2. *Tell your physician when you don't understand what a term means or when you're not clear on how to carry out a prescribed treatment.* It might help to repeat, in your own words, what you thought your physician said out loud to him or her. That way any misunderstandings can be caught quickly before they could be harmful. Most people are very nervous when they are in a physician's office and as a result only remember about half of what they heard. This can be dangerous if the part you forget is critical to your treatment plan. It can also be helpful to *write down any instructions* as your physician gives them to you.

3. *Call your physician if you think of a question at home or if you develop any new symptoms.* Most physicians are willing to answer questions if you call their offices. If he or she can't talk to you when you call, often a staff person will make a note of your question and have the physician call you back. This can save many unnecessary trips to the physician's office! Pharmacists are also willing to answer any questions about medications you may have.

4. *If something is worrying or bothering you, tell your physician about it.* A physician cannot make an accurate diagnosis if he or she doesn't have all the information. Only you know what is going on in your body and how it is different from your previous experiences with your body. So speak up! No problem is "stupid" or "crazy" if it is bothering you.

common stress-related problems

Have you ever had trouble falling asleep? Ever felt worn out before noon? Ever had the "blues" or the "blahs"? If so, this section might give you some new ideas on how to cope with the following problems that are aggravated by stress.

insomnia

Almost everyone has sleep difficulties at some point during their lifetime. Insomnia is the medical term that covers a variety of sleep disturbances. Some people have trouble falling asleep, others may awaken several times during the night, and still others may awaken early in the morning and be unable to fall back to sleep. Insomnia of a chronic kind has afflicted many famous, creative people, including Edgar Allen Poe, Robert Redford, and others. You're in good company while you toss and turn!

The most important thing to remember is that *no one ever died from insomnia*. You may be tired and feel awful, while making everyone around you miserable with your irritability, but your body suffers no real harm. Your body derives almost as much benefit from lying relaxed in your bed as it does from actually sleeping. When your *body and mind* are tired, you *will* sleep.

the real problem

The problem lies in how we *feel* about not sleeping. Most of us have been so well trained that we believe if we don't sleep a full eight hours and then wake up ready to go, there must be something wrong with us. Not so! Not everyone *needs* eight hours of sleep a night. Some people may need more, especially if they are recovering from an illness, engaging in heavy physical activity, or are young. Most people require *less* than eight hours, and you may be one of them. How can you find out how many hours of sleep you need? It's easy—when you are on vacation or have a free weekend, put your watch in a drawer and forget about the time. Go to bed when you feel sleepy (first checking to see what time it is). Sleep until you feel like getting up, and check the time again. If you repeat this experiment for several days, you'll probably begin to see a pattern to the number of hours you really need to sleep. And I'll bet it is less than eight!

It is also rare that people with insomnia get no sleep at all. These people may only remember when they are awake (everyone awakens several times during the course of the night, but since we fall back to sleep quickly, we usually don't remember being awake), their sleep may be unusually light, or they may simply not feel "rested" when they get up, concluding thereby that they haven't slept a wink all night.

the causes

Insomnia can be caused by a wide range of troublemakers—caffeine, too much alcohol, going to bed with a too-full stomach, too much smoking (nicotine in cigarettes acts as a stimulant in our bodies), worrying, a stuffy nose, a scratchy throat, a room that is too warm or too dry, or active physical activity right before going to bed. All these troublemakers act to put your body into high gear and are adequate to keep almost anyone awake and staring at the ceiling.

Our own natural body rhythms can be the culprit as well. Like all the rest of the natural world, human beings run on internal "clocks." These clocks regulate the formation of hormones, determine when we feel hungry, and make us feel sleepy. If you keep track of your energy levels over the course of a few days, you'll probably discover that you have several "sleepy" periods during the course of the day. This is your "prime time" for sleep, and if you don't allow yourself to sleep during your prime time, it may be several hours before your energy cycle comes back around to a drowsy period, making it very difficult for you to fall asleep until then.

Vacations are great times to observe your natural energy cycles. Do what comes naturally. Eat when you are hungry and go to sleep when you are tired. After a couple of days you'll probably notice you eat and go to sleep about the same times every day. These are your prime times for eating and sleeping.

What if your prime times for sleep don't coincide with your job and family responsibilities? I'm a great example of that. My prime time for sleep is between 2 A.M. and 3 A.M. I can drop off easily then and sleep soundly until 8 A.M. But I have to get up by 6 A.M. in order to be at work at 8 A.M. I found that it is possible to reprogram my internal clock, and so can you.

reprogramming

Our bodies seem to thrive on regular schedules, and they adopt habits quickly. Sleeping is no exception. Figure out the number of hours of sleep you need and then backtrack that many hours from the time you need to get up. I need about six hours of sleep but can get by for a while on five. Since I have to get up by 6 A.M., I needed to train myself to get sleepy by midnight. I started following a schedule of going to bed at midnight (even though I wasn't sleepy at first) and getting up at 6 A.M. (even though I had to drag myself out of bed the first few days). Within two weeks my body had adjusted to the new schedule completely. The key is to *stick to the schedule,* even on weekends. Physicians have found that this sort of scheduling can cure even severe sleep problems.

other cures

It can also be helpful to develop a "bedtime ritual" to serve as a cue for your body to begin to prepare for sleep. A ritual can be as simple as reading a book in bed until you feel sleepy (not recommended for students, as this powerful cue can carry over into associations between all kinds of reading and sleep, causing you to nod off over textbooks!), listening to music, taking a bath, or working on a hobby. Watching the

Stress-Related Problems and Disorders

late news on TV isn't highly recommended, for it tends to make people tense rather than helping them relax!

Getting some kind of exercise during the day is also important. When your body is tired, you will sleep. But don't exercise right before bedtime. The initial effect of exercise is that of waking you up, and you want to be able to sleep.

Some people find that a bedtime snack can make them feel drowsy, especially if the snack consists of milk (or milk products) or poultry. The calcium in milk and milk products acts as a mild tranquilizer. Poultry contains a chemical that makes people drowsy (which is why you feel so sleepy after eating turkey on Thanksgiving). So have a chicken sandwich!

If your bedroom is too warm or too dry, your body may have difficulty resting comfortably. Know how difficult it is to sleep on hot summer nights? Our bodies react in the same manner even in the dead of winter if the heat is on full blast and we have piles of blankets and quilts on the bed. Eighty degrees feels the same to your body whether it is caused by summer breezes or too many blankets. A room that is too dry can dehydrate your throat and nose. This discomfort may be keeping you awake. The cure is a humidifier (or bowls of water standing around the bedroom) to add moisture to the air.

If you find that all of these sleep-inducing tricks fail, *get out of bed*. Get up, go to the couch in the living room or the chair in the kitchen, and watch television, read, work on a hobby, or do some chores until you feel drowsy again. If you stay in bed and toss and turn for hours, your mind may begin to associate sleep with stressful situations. Once you begin to do this you've set up a vicious cycle for yourself that is hard to break.

what doesn't work for insomnia

Sleeping pills are *not* an effective cure for insomnia. Over-the-counter sleeping aids usually contain antihistamines (normally used to alleviate symptoms for those who suffer from allergies) or scopolamine (used to handle the symptoms of motion sickness). Both of these medications can make some people drowsy as a side effect, but other people are not affected by them at all.

Prescription sleeping medications are *very* different from over-the-counter sleeping aids. Most prescribed sleeping medications have a sedative or tranquilizing effect and can help people to relax. But our bodies build up a tolerance to these medications very rapidly. Within two weeks it may be necessary to increase the dosage needed to achieve drowsiness. Sleeping pills can also become psychologically addictive in that people may come to believe they cannot sleep on their own without pills and start taking them every night at bedtime whether they actually need them or not.

Prescription sleeping medications can be harmful for another reason as well. When we sleep, we actually cycle through several levels, or stages of sleep. The first stage is a light sleep, which we can awaken from very easily. The other stages are much deeper. It is during these deeper stages that we dream and that our bodies repair and replace cells and tissues to get them ready for another day. The chemicals found in prescription sleeping medications prevent us from reaching those deeper levels of sleep. That's why you can feel groggy in the morning if you took a sleeping pill the night before. Dreams are crucial to your mental health; they allow you to sort through and process all the information you picked up during the course of a day. You especially need time for the repair and building of cells and tissues if your body is coping with the biochemical results of GAS. So for most people, sleeping pills can do more harm than good.

This is not to say that prescription sleeping medications are completely worthless. For some people, under the careful supervision of a physician and for a short period of time, sleeping pills can help provide a sort of "rest" or "oblivion" that may be sorely needed. Examples might be people adjusting to the death of a family member, people suffering pain, or people needing to sleep in a place not conducive to sleep (such as most hospitals). But *sleeping medications should not be used indiscriminately.*

The preceding suggestions have worked for many people. Experiment and find out which "trick" or combination of tricks works best for you. When your body is tired, you will sleep! Look at insomnia as a gift of time to do some of those things you always wanted to do but never found time for during the day!

fatigue

Have you ever felt tired when you got out of bed in the morning? Ever had days when it seemed that all you could do was put one foot in front of the other? Ever fallen asleep while watching the evening news? Chances are you were experiencing fatigue—a very common stress-related problem. Physicians have found that there are three kinds of fatigue—physiological, pathological, and psychological.

physiological fatigue

Physiological fatigue is a symptom of a whole host of physical disorders, ranging from diabetes and infections to heart disease. Some medications have fatigue as a side effect—tranquilizers and sleeping pills can build up in your body, making you feel tired for far longer than might be expected. A deficiency in certain vitamins and minerals can also cause fatigue. Sleeping-pattern changes can cause fatigue as well, as all new mothers and fathers are fully aware.

But the most common cause of physiological fatigue is over-work that tires out the muscles in your body. It results from trying to do too much in too little time. The cure for this kind of physiological fatigue is simple—more sleep. If you *do* get more sleep for a few days and still feel tired, make an appointment with your physician to rule out any other possible physiological cause of fatigue.

pathological fatigue

Pathological fatigue is much rarer. One kind is narcolepsy—an overwhelming and irresistible need for sleep. People suffering from narcolepsy have many "nap attacks" during the course of a day, during which they simply fall asleep wherever they are, whatever they are doing. Another serious problem that causes fatigue is sleep apnea. This is a sleep disorder that causes the sleeper, who is usually a heavy snorer, to stop breathing for up to ninety seconds. He or she then struggles to start breathing again, waking up in the process. Usually people suffering from sleep apnea fall asleep again immediately, but since their sleep has been disturbed, they usually feel very tired the next day, for they are unable to spend enough time in the deeper levels of sleep, where rest really occurs. Finally, deep depression can also cause a person to feel tired. People suffering from a deep depression usually feel very apathetic about life in general and very sad about certain parts of their life. Fatigue goes along with the apathy and sadness. Depression of this kind usually requires a combination of medical and psychological treatment.

psychological fatigue

Psychological fatigue is the most common type of fatigue, however. Stress, anxiety, frustration, anger, and boredom are all the culprits. Boredom in particular can be extremely fatiguing. Research has found that a half hour's worth of boredom can burn up as much energy as a full day's work.

In order for psychological fatigue to be dealt with effectively, its causes have to be confronted and resolved. Confronting the life situations that cause you pain is not easy, but in this case you have to expend some energy in order to get some. You might find it helpful to talk over your concerns with friends of family members. Their help and support might encourage you to change your life situation. Check out what needs you have that aren't being met—and be good to yourself by meeting some of them. You may find that the things you have to deal with can be faced more easily and may even become enjoyable.

If talking things over with friends and trying to meet some of your needs doesn't work, professional help might be in order. Sometimes we can't handle life crises all on our own, and it is okay to seek professionals who make it their business to help other people in times of crisis. A social worker or counselor just might be able to help you get a new perspective on things so that they don't seem so overwhelming.

depression

Many people experience depression when they are under stress. It can range from a case of the "blues" that last a day or so, making you feel sad and weepy, to a full-scale illness that lasts for months, leaving you feeling listless, wrung out, and numb to the joys of life. Depression usually results from some sort of a loss a person experiences. The loss of a role or position in life, the loss of a valued relationship, the loss of a skill or ability, the loss of self-esteem, the loss of public "face," or the loss of a treasured possession can all trigger depression. Even the *imagined* loss of any of these can bring about feelings of depression. Loss can also be cumulative: One loss, or even two, might not bother you, but when the third or fourth one comes along, you feel like you've been hit by a ton of bricks. Most major life changes also involve feelings of depression, which occur just after the big change of some sort is made. This sort of depression is caused by the loss of our old ways of behaving and will subside as we become more comfortable with our new roles and responsibilities.

grief-related depression

It is normal and healthy to grieve over a loss, a loss of any kind, and it is not beneficial to short-cut the grieving process. Unfinished "grief work" tends to crop up later in life, usually when you find yourself under stress again, and compounds that new crisis.

Normal grieving is time limited, usually lasting four to six weeks in its acute phase. Some people may still experience sadness and a sense of loss for up to a year following the death of a family member or close friend. It takes us about that long to say good-bye and restructure our lives after a loss. Don't be concerned if you feel depressed after suffering a loss. The depression is actually *helping* you prepare for a new future.

chronic depression

Some people suffer from depression that lasts longer than a couple of months after a loss, and these people usually benefit from professional counseling. Counseling can help you come to terms with your loss and take your life in hand again. Saying good-bye is never easy.

Lately research has found that people suffering from long-term depression that seems unrelated to a loss may be suffering from a biochemical imbalance of some kind. Various biochemicals present in high concentrations in the brain and body can cause feelings of depression. People with this kind of chronic depression often respond favorably to medications that counteract these biochemicals or keep them from reacting in the brain. The newest research has found that biochemicals produced by our bodies during physical exercise can also counteract the biochemicals causing depression. Running seems to be particularly useful in this case, not only because "happy" biochemicals are produced but because it is easy to record your progress as you begin to run, and that increases your self-confidence.

cures for depression

If you are feeling depressed, take a little time to think about losses you might have experienced in the recent past. Accept the grief process as an important part of mental health and be good to yourself. If you're not sure what caused your depression or if you seem to be "stuck" in the grief process, make an appointment with a mental health professional to talk about it. You don't have to live under gray skies or down in the dumps. Life is too short for that.

headaches

If you are a typical American, there is a high probability you had a headache within the past week. Everybody gets headaches once in a while, and some people get headaches the way other people get "nervous stomachs." These are chronic headache victims. Still fewer people are faced with sometimes incapacitating migraine headaches.

It seems that there are as many causes of headaches as there are people. It is important, therefore, to learn as much as you can about your own headaches in order to figure out how to treat them effectively. You might want to keep a log of your headaches for a few weeks, noting where you are and what you're doing when you notice them, how long they last, what seems to make them better or worse, and what you were thinking or feeling at the time. Then look for patterns. Do your headaches occur in similar situations, at similar times, and so on?

simple headaches

Simple headaches can be caused by any one of the following: sore throat; eye strain; fever; anemia; muscle spasm; holding your head at an odd angle for a long period of time; fatigue; squinting; allergies to foods and airborn particles; sodium nitrite (found in bacon, hot dogs, luncheon meats, and so forth); too much sun; monosodium glutamate (MSG for short, often found in Chinese food and used as a flavor enhancer); chocolate; caffeine; and cigarette smoke. Headaches caused by these culprits are easily cured once you change your habits, get some sleep, take care of the original health problem, or discontinue eating the offending food.

tension headaches

Most people suffering from headaches have "tension" headaches, which are caused by muscle contractions. These muscle contractions can be triggered by stress or a specific problem. You can distinguish this type of headache easily for yourself. Tension headaches usually affect both sides of your head, may be felt across your forehead or down your neck as well, and happen again and again. Once you are able to pinpoint what triggers these tension headaches, you can take steps to remedy the situation. If you can do that, you will usually find that your headaches will go away without professional help.

depression headaches

Some people who have chronic headaches may have a "masked" or hidden depression, which shows up as headaches. People with depression headaches usually notice that their headaches are worse early in the morning and again late in the afternoon. Often there are other symptoms as well: You may awaken early in the morning and be unable to go back to sleep; backaches or chest pains may be a problem; you may suddenly cry for no apparent reason; or your behavior may change—a person who loves to eat may stop eating, or a usually neat person will let his or her appearance go. Depression headaches are best treated by a physician and mental health professional together. A counselor can help you uncover and resolve the situation causing your depression, while a physician might recommend the use of an antidepressant drug for a short period of time to break the headache cycle.

migraine headaches

Other people suffer from migraines, and most of these sufferers are women. Migraine headaches tend to affect only one side of your head at a time; can cause nausea, vomiting, and loss of appetite; may be preceded by an "aura" (flashing lights across your field of vision, numbness in arms or legs, a taste in your mouth, or a noticeable odor); and seem to run in families.

Physicians used to believe that people who got migraine headaches were perfectionists who worked hard to maintain their high internal standards of behavior. But recent research has found that migraines affect people with the entire spectrum of personality characteristics.

It has been found that careful control of your diet can help control migraines. Aged cheese, fermented wines or liquors, chocolate, nuts, monosodium glutamate, and nitrites have all been shown to be capable of triggering migraine attacks. The level of sugar in your blood may also play a part: Drastic changes in blood sugar levels can also trigger migraines. If you eat balanced meals three times a day, which will keep your blood sugar level fairly stable, you may be able to prevent some migraine attacks.

Changes in the weather, altitude, sleeping habits, and relaxation patterns can also trigger migraine headaches. Some migraine sufferers notice that they get severe headaches on the weekend. This may be caused by changes in eating, sleeping, and relaxation patterns followed during the work week. The key here is to keep your body on a regular schedule, even during the weekends.

A serious problem can arise when women who get migraines take birth control pills. The hormones in birth control pills have been found to increase the frequency, severity, and duration of migraine headaches. If you are presently taking birth control pills and are experiencing headaches that resemble migraines, it might be a good idea to check with your physician. Switching to an alternative method of birth control has relieved considerable suffering for many women migraine sufferers.

Physicians have a variety of medications available to help eliminate very severe migraine problems. The most widely prescribed are ergotamine tartarate and propanolol hydrochloride. Ergotamine tartarate is taken at the first sign of a migraine attack in order to stop it, while propanolol hydrochloride is usually taken on a regular basis to prevent migraines.

cures for tension headaches

If you have a "garden variety" tension headache, the following tips might help you make it more bearable, if not get rid of it entirely.

1. *When you first become aware of your headache, check to see if muscles in your jaw, forehead, neck, or shoulders are tense.* Consciously relaxing or massaging these muscles may relieve your headache.

2. *Heat, cold, or steam can ease the pain of a headache.* Heat and steam (standing over a sink of hot water with a towel over your head to trap the steam) are particularly effective in relaxing tense muscles and in easing sinus congestion. Heating pads placed on the back of your neck or on sore shoulders can also relax tense muscles. Cold compresses can help make a hangover bearable. Experiment to see which approach works best for you.

3. *Try an over-the-counter (OTC) pain reliever, but choose carefully and use wisely.* There is a wide variety of pain relievers available OTC. The buffering agents added to some pain relievers have not been proven to be very effective, and plain aspirin taken with a glass of milk or lots of water appears to work just as well and costs much less.

4. *Aspirin is aspirin, whether it comes in a fancy package or a*

plain bottle. Higher prices don't necessarily mean higher quality; they usually mean more advertising and fancier packaging. Check prices and purchase the brand that costs less per tablet. Aspirin can decompose rapidly when exposed to air. If your aspirin smells like vinegar, throw it out! It has begun to decompose and is no longer effective in relieving pain. Unless you get many headaches, buy smaller packages of aspirin tablets. That way the tablets won't begin to decompose before you can use them up.

5. *Be knowledgeable about nonaspirin pain relievers.* Nonaspirin pain relievers usually contain acetaminophen as their major ingredient. If you are allergic to aspirin or find that aspirin irritates your stomach, you might want to consider trying an acetaminophen-based pain reliever. However, acetaminophen is *not* effective in reducing inflammation (such as that found in arthritis, joint injuries, and so on), while aspirin can be helpful in reducing that kind of inflammation. If you need an anti-inflammatory medication and cannot tolerate aspirin, your physician can prescribe a variety of such agents.

Recently it was discovered that people can overdose on acetaminophen, particularly if they have liver-disease damage. Acetaminophen is broken down in the liver, and if your body takes in more of the drug than your liver can handle, damage can result. As long as you follow the instructions provided on the pain reliever bottle and take no more tablets per day than are recommended, you will not overdose, providing you have no liver problems. But never take more than the recommended daily amount, because acetaminophen overdoses are difficult to diagnose and treat.

6. *More pain reliever does not necessarily mean better pain relief.* Don't take more aspirin or nonaspirin pain reliever than is recommended every four hours. More aspirin (or its substitute) does *not* mean more pain relief. Aspirin does not eliminate pain, it only raises your tolerance of pain. Aspirin can only raise your tolerance level a given amount anyway, which is usually very limited. If the recommended dose of a pain reliever doesn't seem to work for you, *see your physician.* The pain may be masking an underlying problem, or you may need a prescription pain reliever.

7. *Many pain relievers have caffeine added to them.* Caffeine was added on the theory that it would "speed relief through your bloodstream." Recent research has found that caffeine doesn't work that way and that it may not be effective at all in hastening pain relief. If you feel that the addition of caffeine does make your headaches go away faster, you might want to consider taking regular aspirin with tea, coffee, or cola drinks. All these contain caffeine and are usually cheaper in the long run than paying for higher priced pain relievers that have caffeine already added to them.

dysfunctional eating

Many people tend to overeat when they are under stress. Our culture also at times seems to be obsessed with thinness, and when overeating as a response to stress piles on the pounds, we can be put in an even more stressful situation.

Overeating is not inherently bad, if practiced with some moderation. It is important to assess your eating patterns to see what your overeating is telling you about your needs, values, and life situation. Ask yourself the following questions.

1. *Is there a risk to your health caused by overeating?* Is your overweight problem severe; do you have high blood pressure diabetes, for example? If you don't have any serious risks to your health from being overweight, "dysfunctional" eating is probably the least harmful of the ineffective coping techniques people use that will be talked about in this chapter.

2. *Is there a pattern to your overeating?* Check out the times, places, situations, and your feelings when you overeat. Can this information tell you about the ways to control parts of your life that are stressful for you?

3. *Do you have favorite stress foods that you consistently binge on?* What kinds of foods are they? Do you prepare them yourself or are they "fast foods"? Are they "comfort foods" from your childhood— foods you associate with nurturing and being comforted? Are they

"lucky" or "magic" foods, like chicken soup? What do they tell you about your needs? Chewy foods may signify that you have a problem you need to chew on for a while. Crunchy foods might indicate that you'd like to bite somebody's head off! Mushy foods may mean you'd like to be taken care of for a while.

4. *Do you otherwise eat a diet adequate in nutrition?* If your overall diet is balanced, occasional binges are okay. If you can't get goodies from other people when you need them, you can behave responsibly by preparing them for yourself. Choclate chip cookies (my favorite binge food!) may not solve any problems, but they sure make them more palatable!

5. *Could something else more "healthy" be an effective substitute if you consistently binge on junk foods?* You can get clues to this from the texture, manner of preparation, and taste of your binge foods. Experiment and see what works for you. It's important not to berate yourself for overconsumption of healthy foods when you are under stress. You don't need to add to your already high stress level.

The goal here is *moderation.* As long as overeating is not causing you any serious health problems and is serving as an effective crutch, *use the crutch!* Teddy bears are crutches, too, but nearly everyone outgrows them when their life situations change. The same holds true for overeating. When things in your life straighten out, it is a good possibility you will cut back on your overeating without even realizing it.

If you have become bothered by your weight caused by overeating while you are under stress, it is important to sort through your feelings about your weight and what that means for you. It is not always wise to begin a diet when you are experiencing stress in other areas of your life. Most diets started when people are under stress don't succeed, simply because food serves as a good relaxer. So ask yourself the following questions before you start dieting:

1. Why do I feel upset about my eating patterns and weight? What is it about my situation that is upsetting to me?

2. What values do I have about my weight and overeating?

3. What are my reasons for wanting to start a diet?

4. Are these reasons realistic? (For example, losing fifteen pounds most likely will *not* change your life dramatically, pick up your sex life, make you witty and interesting, or cause someone to fall madly in love with you.)

5. What functions are my eating patterns serving for me? What substitutes can I find for these functions?

If you feel that an important stress area for you is your weight, by all means practice cutting back on your eating and start on a sensible, safe diet and exercise program. Be good to yourself while you are dieting. Remember that you are already under stress, so try not to create too much more stress for yourself!

If you have tried various diets in the past that haven't worked for you and this causes you to experience stress, take heart. The most recent research on obesity has exposed some startling new facts. Researchers have found that people who are up to 20 percent overweight (as based on the standard weight tables set up by insurance companies) run no real risk to their health. For example, if the weight tables say you should weigh between 120 and 140 because you are 5 feet 6 inches tall, and you weigh 159 (like me), the researchers feel that that level of weight is within the safe range for healthy Americans. They've also found that if you have stayed at your present weight for several years, chances are that that is the weight that is best for *your body*—particularly if you eat balanced meals and don't snack a lot between meals. The researchers recommend accepting the fact that your body is the way it is (because of your heredity, biochemistry, and fat cells) and quit berating yourself because you aren't model-skinny. Perhaps your body was never *meant* to be model-skinny. In other words, if you feel good at your present weight and have no serious health problems, quit worrying about your weight. These same researchers also found that people who were in that 20 percent overweight range survived surgery better, recuperated from infections faster, produced healthier babies, and actually lived longer than people who were at the "correct" weight or under it. Now, if we could just get the fashions to change! (However, there is already a trend by haute couture designers to design clothes for women who wear larger than a size 12, and magazines geared toward larger sized people are appearing on the newsstands.)

caffeine consumption

Caffeine is present in coffee, tea, colas, and some over-the-counter pain relievers. Chocolate contains a substance that also acts like a stimulant in our bodies. In *large* amounts, caffeine can cause nervousness, extra production of acid in the stomach, and insomnia. The amount that will cause these reactions varies from person to person, depending upon how sensitive you are to caffeine. Some people can drink lots of coffee and drop right off to sleep, whereas others have a cup of coffee at dinner and are awake all night. You might want to experiment to see what your personal tolerance level is for caffeine.

Caffeine levels vary, too, in tea, coffee, and colas. The following list (put together by *Consumer Reports*) provides rough estimates of the amount of caffeine found in each:

- Brewed coffee—100–150 milligrams per 6-ounce cup (*not* a mug!).
- Instant coffee—86–99 milligrams per 6-ounce cup.
- Brewed tea—60–75 milligrams per 6-ounce cup.
- Cola drinks—40–60 milligrams per 12-ounce serving.
- Pain relievers—32 milligrams per tablet or more (check the ingredients list on the bottle for an accurate measure).
- Decaffeinated coffee or tea—some brands have 1–2 milligrams per 6-ounce serving, but check the label to be sure.

Instant tea has slightly less caffeine than brewed tea, and herbal teas can contain caffeine, so it's important to read the ingredients label on all beverage packages to be sure.

If you are a heavy caffeine consumer and want to decrease your intake, follow these simple steps.

1. *Don't stop cold turkey.* Your body has become dependent upon caffeine as a stimulant and has established a biochemical balance that takes the high levels of caffeine into account. To reduce withdrawal symptoms (usually tiredness, headaches, irritability) and increase your chances of sticking with your resolution to cut back, you need to *wean yourself away gradually,* in the same way you got started. To do this, you might keep track of how many cups of coffee or tea you consume daily, then cut back on one or two cups a day for the first week, three cups the second week, four cups the third week, and so on. It is not actually necessary to eliminate caffeine entirely. Scientists say that humans can usually tolerate 350–500 milligrams of caffeine per day without any severe side effects. So unless you are extremely sensitive to caffeine or are under a physician's orders to eliminate your caffeine intake completely, you need not cut coffee and tea entirely out of your diet—just cut back!

2. *Because having a "cup of something" in front of you can be soothing and a tough habit to break, you might want to try a substitute.* Try tea, cocoa, instant coffee or tea, decaffeinated tea or coffee— any beverage with a lower caffeine level than the one you are presently consuming. This way you will gradually get used to the taste as well.

Many coffee drinkers say that tea tastes like "warm dishwater," but a few teas have a robust flavor that coffee drinkers might like. Some teas to try are English breakfast tea, orange pekoe tea blends, orange pekoe and pekoe cut black tea blends, Irish breakfast tea, Morning Thunder or Roastaroma by Celestial Seasonings, and Early Riser by Bigelow Teas.

If you are a heavy tea drinker, you might want to switch to instant tea (as I did) or experiment with the new decaffeinated teas that are available in some areas. I have tried a few and didn't care much for them, but many of my friends and students in my stress management classes swear by them.

Many people are making the switch to herbal teas and herbal tea blends. Many of these teas contain no caffeine, and are therefore good substitutes for beverages with high caffeine levels. But a few words of caution are in order: Make sure you purchase your herbal teas from a reputable dealer; make the tea weak at first until you get used to it; don't overdo a good thing—some herbs in high concentration can cause diarrhea and stomach upset. Also, some people, especially people with allergies to various grasses and weeds, are sensitive to herbal teas. Once again, moderation is the key. Don't suddenly substitute twenty cups of herbal tea for your usual twenty cups of coffee. Your body will put up one heck of a fight! Listen to what your body is telling you.

smoking and drinking

Essentially, what holds true for caffeine holds true for smoking and drinking. Both only become problems when they negatively affect your life-style, health, or responsibilities.

While they are not terribly great for you, smoking and drinking don't seem to do that much harm if done in moderation. If you are concerned about smoking or drinking too much, ask yourself the following questions:

1. Is there a risk to your health or life-style from the smoking/drinking pattern you've established?
2. Is there a pattern to your overconsumption of cigarettes or alcohol?
3. Can you use a less harmful substitute for the alcohol or cigarettes?
4. What needs do alcohol or cigarettes fill for you? Can you find other ways to meet these needs?

There are several schools of thought on the right way and the wrong way to go about reducing your cigarette or alcohol intake. For smokers, the most recent research seems to support the notion of stopping cold turkey. This study found that people who stop cold turkey suffer *less* in the long run than people who gradually cut back, and they tend to stick to their resolve not to smoke anymore longer than do people who wean themselves away from cigarettes. You need to experiment for yourself and see which way works best for you. If you simply cannot quit smoking, at least consider switching to one of the new low-tar or tobacco-free cigarettes that are on the market. At least you will be doing less harm to your body.

If you have a serious problem with drinking, the most successful way to quit is to get professional help, either from a peer-group program such as Alcoholics Anonymous or from professional mental health practitioners. If you have been drinking heavily for a long period of time, your body needs special care while you quit drinking, and you'll find the support and encouragement you receive in an organized program to be very helpful. If you're a social drinker and are concerned about drinking more and enjoying it less, you might want to try the following suggestions.

1. *Try alternatives to hard liquor.* Wine has a lower alcoholic content than distilled alcoholic beverages, and physicians have found that moderate wine consumption (one or two 6-ounce glasses) before and/or during dinner can help people relax, can perk up poor appetites, and can aid digestion. "Coolers" or "spritzers" (soda plus wine, liqueurs or liquor) can give you a "tall" drink that lasts longer when you sip it. People find that a single cooler will adequately take the place of two or three normal drinks at a party.

2. *Try the new nonalcoholic party drinks available in many bars and restaurants.* Nonalcoholic mixed drinks are no longer limited to the wretched "Shirley Temple," as many establishments are producing a varied array of tasty, exotic drinks without a drop of alcohol. My favorite hangout has come up with a whole list of approximately ten different nonalcoholic drinks—everything from strawberry daiquiris and piña coladas without rum to hot spiced drinks during the winter.

3. *Become terribly chic and order bottled mineral water.* Most restaurants offer a selection of bottled mineral waters, including the ubiquitous Perrier, and it is currently "in" to order mineral water with a slice of lemon. You can be terribly avant-garde and ask to have it with a slice of lime. Many people I know are also offering bottled mineral

water at parties as an option to drinks or wine, and it is indeed a very festive alternative.

4. *Rely on the "tried and true" nonalcoholic beverages.* There's nothing wrong with asking for a lemon-lime soft drink, cola, ginger ale, or fruit juice. I've begun to notice that it is becoming more and more acceptable for people to ask for these traditional nonalcoholic drinks, especially at lunches and dinners or at get-togethers after work, when you have to drive home in rush-hour traffic.

stress and sex

Current permissive and open attitudes about sex and sexuality have certainly cleared cobwebs from the corners of our minds. But this same permissiveness and openness has added anxiety and stress to our approach to sex.

With the increased knowledge of sex and sexual activities came an assumption (or in some cases, an expectation) that now everyone should be a superb sexual performer. Now we worry not only about how our partner is responding but also about whether or not we are performing or responding correctly. Partners worry about the length, intensity, type, and timing of orgasms. Magazines, books, and films tell us we are capable of multiple orgasms, and many people are beginning to wonder if something is wrong if they don't achieve them. Add to this scenario increasing pressures from work, new problems managing home and family tasks while working, and guilt for just about everything else. The result is an explosive situation for stress overload.

Stress reduces our ability to become aroused sexually. Because we only have a limited amount of energy available at any one time, having much of that energy drained away with worry or anxiety effectively *reduces* the amount of energy to use in other ways, including sex. Since time immemorial (partly for survival reasons), one of the first areas to suffer from "energy cutbacks" has been sexual responsiveness. If you can't become aroused, you can't respond. It's that simple.

Our society also places great value on "being in control" of our feelings. This is a paradox of sorts. We're expected to be repressed in all areas of our emotional lives except in sexual relationships. Once we learn too well how to control our feelings, we become afraid to "let loose," even during sex. Another problem is that bottled-up emotions usually have to come out somewhere, and when they do, they very often affect sexual arousal, response, and performance.

Having had training and experience in sexuality counseling, I've seen how disastrous this whole idea of "sexual performance" can be for people. I have found that it is *very rare* for a person *never* to experience difficulties in sexual relationships due to stress. *Almost everyone will experience some kind of stress-related sexual problem at some time during his or her life.* This "normal" stress reaction can be compounded if we begin to worry about our problem of arousal or responsiveness. If we worry too much, it will be even *harder* to respond, and a vicious cycle can begin.

How can these stress-related sexual problems be solved? Actually, most solve themselves once we eliminate the idea of "performance." I find the idea of "pleasuring" much more conducive to arousal and response. "Pleasuring" involves understanding that sex does not ultimately need to result in intercourse and mutual orgasm in order to be enjoyable and fun. If you believe that sex must *always* result in intercourse and orgasm, you're missing out on a whole lot of fun. "Sex" also includes hugging, kissing, stroking, caressing, massaging, talking, and so on. These activities can be enjoyable ends in themselves, not just means to an end.

More truthful, realistic information can also be helpful. Unfortunately, most of the "information" available in the media is based on fantasy, with very little relation to what goes on in most people's lives. It is a wonderful fantasy that people are always thinking about sex, are always ready for sex, and always perform superbly when they engage in sex. But that's just what it is—*fantasy.* People also think about bills; worry about responsibilities and obligations; agonize over courses, exams, reports, business deals, and budgets; fear inflation—and sometimes cannot respond sexually because of this. That is normal, that is real life (as opposed to "reel" life), and that is okay.

It is also true that men and women respond differently and require different things in order to become aroused, mainly as a result of our socialization process. That's normal, and that's okay, too. It could be helpful for partners to learn more about how men and women respond sexually, and the last chapter of this book lists some well-written, accurate books you might want to explore.

It is also helpful for partners to discuss together how important sex is for them and how they want to arrange their lives to spend time together. I've found that most people become aroused more easily and are more responsive sexually when their relationship with their sexual partner involves more than just sex—when the partners share similar interests, spend time together apart from sexual activity, and are understanding of each other's needs and preferences. If that sounds hopelessly old-fashioned and "out of date," so be it! But I think our elders can still teach us a thing or two about love and loving.

Eliminating the notion of "performance" from sexual encounters greatly reduces the potential for stress overload. One of the best ways to do this is to become familiar with a technique called sensate focusing, which is often used in sexual therapy. Sensate focusing involves becoming aware of all the areas of our bodies that are erogenous—in fact, our entire body is capable of being an "erogenous zone" if we let it. The following steps, based on sensate focusing, can help you become more aware of how your body responds and then becomes aroused. And remember, this does not have to lead to intercourse to be pleasurable and fulfilling. (If you want to go all the way, fine, but it's not necessary.)

1. Start by taking a long, warm bath or shower. (Together with your partner if you enjoy that. Some people don't, and that's okay.)

2. Turn down the lights, lock the doors, put on some soft music, open a bottle of wine. Give yourself and your partner time to unwind, relax, and turn off the worries of the day. If you have children, it might be helpful to wait until they're asleep. Or ask a friend or baby-sitter to care for them while you and your partner go to a hotel, motel, or a friend's cabin or cottage. The goal is to prevent interruptions, or the worry about potential interruptions. Even putting a latch on the inside of your bedroom door and unplugging the phone can help.

3. When you and your partner are relaxed and feeling good, climb into bed, first taking off robes, nightgowns, pajamas, and so on. Flip a coin or draw straws to see who gets a chance to be pleasured first.

4. Once the first pleasuree has been chosen, go over the ground rules. No direct stimulation of the breasts, nipples, or genitals at first, just focus on exploring other parts of the body. The pleasuree is to give the pleasurer feedback on what feels good, what would feel better, and what doesn't feel so good. Remember, we can't read each other's minds, no matter how well we know each other, so it is important to ask for what you want. The pleasuree is to return the pleasure by pleasuring the partner in turn.

5. Now comes the fun part! The pleasurer begins caressing, stroking, touching, and exploring the pleasuree's body—everywhere. That includes the pleasuree's neck, shoulders, back, tummy, legs, thighs, arms, lips, ears, eyelids, face, scalp, toes, fingers, and so on. Some people like to use lotions or creams to make the caressing and massaging smoother. Others find such lotions messy and might want to try baby powder or dusting powder instead. Such powders can also act as lubricants and reduce friction. The pleasurer doesn't have to rely just on his or her fingers and hands to caress and touch. Experiment with your tongue, lips, toes, legs, eyelashes, and so forth. Tiny kisses on the inner thigh or eyelash "tickles" on the face can feel fantastic! Flavored lotions are also available, should you decide to really experiment.

6. The pleasuree should keep the pleasurer aware of what feels good and what doesn't feel good. If you want your pleasurer to touch you somewhere else or do something differently, that's okay. Just say so!

7. The pleasuree may want to have his or her breasts, nipples, or genitals stroked or caressed. That is okay, *after* other areas of the body have been explored. But try to refrain from actual intercourse, at least

at first. As you become more aware of the various ways to pleasure each other, you may want to explore alternative ways to caress, touch, or massage each other's breasts, nipples, and genitals. Remember, you don't have to rely just on your fingers and hands. Experiment with using your lips, tongue, eyelashes, legs, and so on here as well.

8. Believe it or not, the pleasuree will reach a point at which he or she is satisfied and content. Then it's the pleasuree's turn to please the pleasurer, making sure to follow the same guidelines previously listed. You will probably find that it is just as much fun to give pleasure as it is to receive it!

9. Some people may have difficulty accepting pleasure from their partner. In this case it is helpful for them to do the pleasuring first, allowing them to become more comfortable with receiving pleasure by first experiencing what it is like to give pleasure.

10. If you or your partner have difficulty "getting into" sensate focusing at first, that is okay. We're not taught much about how our bodies and emotions react to this sort of activity, and the new feelings you might experience can be a little "scary" or "weird" at first. That's normal, just go slowly and only go as far as you feel comfortable. As you become more comfortable with caressing and being caressed, you will discover that you have erogenous zones where you never even knew they existed!

Very few people need sex therapy. I've found that if couples give themselves some time away from "performing" and focus on "pleasuring" while they sort out other stressful parts of their lives, most sexual-response-and-arousal problems take care of themselves. If this *doesn't* work, it tells me that there may be a relationship problem the couple needs to confront and work out. In this case, assistance from a mental health professional is very helpful. Only people with very severe sexual problems need the assistance of a sex therapist, and that help is most useful after assistance from mental health professionals has been found to be insufficient.

what doesn't work

It is now time for the only "sermon" you will find in this book. It is also time for me to outline one of my major biases. I am very strongly opposed to adding unnecessary chemicals and drugs to human bodies, especially when this represents an attempt to cope with stress. There are two reasons for this: first, most of the time drugs do not work in alleviating stress; and second, *any* drug is potentially harmful. When people ask me what I have to say about using drugs to cope with stress, I always say I can sum it up in one word—*don't*. And I mean it!

tranquilizers

Tranquilizers are the most overprescribed category of drugs in the world. Several years ago researchers estimated that 140 million new prescriptions (not refills) were written each year for tranquilizers. And women are far more likely to get prescriptions for tranquilizers than men.

Both the physician and the patient are at fault when it comes to tranquilizer abuse. Physicians are often "too busy" to help a patient solve the causes of his or her stress, often lack adequate training in human behavior and personality development and intervention techniques, or are uninformed about alternative coping techniques. Once physicians graduate from medical school and become busy seeing patients, they get most of their information on new developments in health care courtesy of drug companies, which spend millions of dollars each year putting out slick, colorful, "educational" materials for busy physicians. This "educational" material is also almost always related in some way to drugs the companies have for sale, so it is not surprising that physicians prescribe lots of drugs. Unfortunately people involved in alternative ways of coping with illness and stress don't have the big advertising budgets drug companies have, but through seminars and courses in medical schools, people involved in alternative coping techniques are slowly informing physicians about nondrug options. But that takes time—lots of it.

Patients who don't ask for alternatives or don't talk about the stresses behind their symptoms are equally guilty. The "I don't want to take responsibility for my pain—just give me a pill to make it go away" mentality is a result of our culture's preference for instant cures and instant relief. But stress *cannot* be removed or relieved instantly.

Tranquilizers are usually ineffective in reducing stress because they do nothing to solve the problems that caused the stress in the first place. They just make your brain numb. By numbing your brain, they reduce anxiety that is needed as an impetus to begin working on the problems and resolving the stresses.

Human beings' tolerance of tranquilizers increases rapidly, meaning that it takes more of the drug to get the same effect. Some tranquilizers are physically addictive, but *all* are psychologically addictive. And withdrawal from tranquilizers is a long, unpleasant, difficult process.

This is not to say that tranquilizers are completely worthless. In certain situations—such as death of a spouse or family member, coping with the immediate effects of a disaster or a disease, or in the treatment of high blood pressure and other chronic diseases—tranquilizers do have a role to play. But only for a short, limited period of time under a physician's careful supervision. Remember, tranquilizers are drugs, and they are drugs that can be deadly if abused.

sleeping pills

Sleeping pills are probably the second most abused prescription drug in the United States. The problem with prescription sleeping medications is that they don't really help you sleep, they only provide oblivion for a period of time. The chemicals present in these medications prevent you from reaching the deeper levels of sleep during which you dream and your body repairs tissue damage and replaces worn-out cells. Dreaming is important for mental health. We sort through and process all the information we've been exposed to during the day. Feelings are analyzed and processed as well. We also need to have cells replaced and tissues repaired as a process of living.

Our tolerance of prescription sleeping medications increases rapidly. We need increasing amounts of the drug to produce the desired results. Some physicians contend that after two weeks of continuous use, sleeping pills, in *any* amount, are no longer effective in inducing sleep. Their only value is as a placebo.

Sleep-inducing drugs are psychologically addictive as well, and withdrawal is a lengthy, agonizing process. Because they can interact with other medications, prescription sleeping medications can precipitate adverse reactions and can cause death.

Once again, this is not to say that sleep-inducing medications are without usefulness. Prescription medications may be helpful in times of crisis or to break a stubborn cycle of insomnia. But they should be used only for a limited period of time under the strict supervision of a physician—with careful regulation of any additional medications or alcohol use.

amphetamines

Amphetamines, or "uppers," are also widely abused. Many people have gotten prescriptions for amphetamines to help them lose weight or cope with fatigue. Unfortunately, amphetamines help with *neither* in the long run. Amphetamines have not been proven effective in weight reduction, and any "lift" in feelings of fatigue is usually temporary. These drugs can be physically as well as psychologically addictive, and withdrawal is a lengthy, painful process. Dependence on "uppers" often fosters the dependence on sleeping pills as well, in an effort to "come down" off the amphetamines so that a person can sleep. This leads to a vicious cycle of uppers to wake up and sleeping pills to sleep. Withdrawal from this kind of double-drug dependence is even more difficult and unpleasant.

There is a place for amphetamines in psychiatric medicine, albeit a small one. They can be useful in breaking the cycle of chronic fatigue or depression complicated by severe fatigue. But amphetamines should only be used for a short period of time under the strict guidance of a psychiatrist or physician.

antidepressant and mood-altering drugs

Antidepressant medications are less abused in our society, only because they are somewhat harder to obtain. Antidepressant drugs should *not* be used as an occasional "pick-me-up." They are a serious medication for serious conditions. They won't cure "the blues," either.

Antidepressants can be useful for certain psychiatric conditions, such as psychotic depressions (severe depressions lasting for months with deep apathy and fatigue) and manic-depressive illnesses (in which people swing from tremendous emotional highs to devastating emotional lows in a cyclical pattern). But they don't take effect immediately. It may be several weeks before improvement is noticed, and they require careful regulation by a physician or psychiatrist for maximum effectiveness.

mind-altering drugs

These drugs were very popular in the 1960s and early 1970s, but their use appears to be on the decrease presently. This category includes marijuana, LSD, STP, Quaaludes, heroin, morphine, and so on. The major problem with these drugs is that they are, for the most part, extremely physically, as well as psychologically, addictive. Tolerance of them increases very rapidly, and they interact with other drugs to cause potentially lethal reactions. Withdrawal is very painful and lengthy.

They are also almost impossible to get legally without a prescription, which means that they usually must be purchased on the street. The quality of street drugs varies enormously, and a buyer can never be certain of the dosage or purity of his or her purchase. As a result, street drugs are frequently deadly.

People react differently to mind-altering drugs, and individual reactions even vary from use to use. You can *never* be sure of the outcome when you use such drugs.

Morphine does have a role to play in pain reduction. It has been found to be helpful for people suffering great pain, particularly pain caused by diseases such as cancer. Codeine is used to lessen pain from surgery or other medical conditions. But these drugs are never completely safe, even under the supervision of a physician. They are best used for short periods of time with extremely careful control by a physician.

Marijuana is the object of great controversy. Initially researchers thought it was relatively "safe," but more recent research has begun to uncover potential risks for long-term use. "Pot" is also psychologically addictive, and its use can be an extremely difficult habit to break. Purchased on the street, its strength and purity cannot be assured, and it is illegal in most places to grow your own. Marijuana is *not* effective in reducing stress, since it acts in the same way tranquilizers do, to mask stress-producing problems, not solve them.

Marijuana has only two uses for which its effectiveness has been documented. It has been found useful in the treatment of various eye diseases related to increasing pressure of the fluid inside the eye. It also seems to help reduce the nausea that is a common side effect of chemotherapy treatments for cancer. In many states even medical use of marijuana for these purposes is illegal.

Cocaine is another drug that was once considered to be relatively harmless. Sigmund Freud was one of many who promoted its use. Recent research has proven, however, that it is psychologically addictive and can also react with other drugs to cause potentially lethal combinations. In addition, when sniffed through the nose (or "snorted"), cocaine destroys the membranes and tissues that make up the nose. Complicated reconstructive surgery may be necessary to rebuild damaged nasal passages.

a final word on things that don't work

In conclusion, it seems that drugs of any kind have the potential for far more harm than any good they can do in treating stress-related problems and disorders. They are not to be taken lightly. The drugs mentioned earlier do not relieve stress, so why use them? There is a whole smorgasbord of techniques and tricks that are safer and far more effective. The next several chapters explore those techniques.

5

anger, communication, and assertiveness

This chapter deals with three typically high-stress areas in most people's lives—anger, communication, and assertiveness. Anger—how we express it and cope with it—often poses problems for effective communication and expression of assertiveness, so it will be discussed first. I think it is essential to understand how effective communication works in order to appreciate assertiveness techniques, so communication will be covered second and assertiveness will be discussed last.

how anger works

When do you get angry? What happens when you get angry? How do you feel? Most of the time "anger" happens so fast to us that we don't have a clear picture of how anger progresses. We've also been taught as children that anger is "bad." So that when we get angry, we can also get upset about the fact that we are angry! However, there is a definite cycle leading to the expression of anger, and if we know how that cycle works, we can also learn how to circumvent ineffective expressions of anger.

In the initial phase of the anger cycle, a person is confronted with a situation that poses a threat to him or her in some way, or that frustrates attempts to get needs met. In my work as a therapist, I've seen that there are six possible kinds of situations that can pose this sort of threat to people.

1. *Loss of self-esteem.* This kind of loss is felt most keenly internally. We feel we have failed somehow or that we have "let ourselves down."

2. *Loss of face.* This loss is felt most keenly publicly. Our friends and family may have learned about a failure or inadequacy of ours, or the image of ourselves we present to society has been tarnished in some way.

3. *Threat of physical violence or harm.* Our self-preservation instinct comes in here.

4. *Loss of valued possession(s).* When an object we value is taken away from us, we can feel threatened because of the hassle involved in replacing the object, the pain of readjusting our lives if the object cannot be replaced, or simply because of the emotional investment we have in the object. The same things hold true for valued skills and abilities.

5. *Loss of a valued role.* We define ourselves to society and our own selves in terms of the various roles we play in society. Since most of our identity is based on these roles, losing a role is very painful. If the role we lose is important to our lives and society, we can feel worthless and "faceless."

6. *Loss of valued relationship.* Relationships with others are very important to most people, and losing a valued relationship—especially

if you don't think you can find an alternative way to meet your needs formerly fulfilled by the lost relationship—can be very painful and threatening.

In the few seconds that it takes your brain to register the loss/threat or potential loss/threat in the situation in front of you, your brain also conducts a "power analysis." A power analysis includes an evaluation of the type and severity of the threat/loss posed to you by the initial situation and an analysis of the resources you have available to deal with this situation. If your power analysis is positive, meaning that either the potential threat/loss is not great or you can survive even if the threat/loss is serious (meaning you have enough resources to get you through the crisis), you will not get angry, and the anger cycle ends here. If, however, your power analysis comes up negative— meaning that either the situation poses a severe threat/loss to you or you do not have adequate resources to deal with the threat/loss—angry feelings will be triggered.

What happens when angry feelings are triggered? Individual reactions depend upon both the outcome of the power analysis and the person's personality, but some common reactions to angry feelings follow.

1. *Inability to talk or express angry feelings.* When I am really angry, for example, I simply cannot talk. No words come out, no matter how hard I try. When I am "moderately to really" angry, I can talk, but the words come out very softly, slowly, and clearly. My family and friends know that when I sound that way, I am furious, but people who don't know me well don't believe I am really angry, and that can cause problems.

2. *Withdrawal.* This involves giving someone you're angry at the "silent treatment" or withdrawing physically or mentally from the situation itself.

3. *Avoidance or distraction.* Some people go to great lengths to avoid situations that could lead to angry feelings or try to turn attention elsewhere to distract themselves and others from angry feelings.

4. *"Blowing up."* Some people yell, scream, shout, kick, hurt, fight, stomp their feet, or even kill when they get angry.

5. *Practicing "passive-aggressive" behaviors.* People who use passive-aggressive behaviors look, at least on the outside, as if they are going along with the situation and are not angry. But beneath the surface they are planning and executing all sorts of dirty "sneak attacks" to get back at the others involved in the situation. The sneak attacks are usually the little things that irritate the other people the most.

6. *Internalizing the anger.* People who internalize anger literally "swallow" it, they turn their anger inward and develop psychosomatic symptoms and problems.

7. *Panic.* Many people literally panic when they get angry. They are so frightened of their own anger that they get scared and confused.

8. *Projecting anger onto others.* People who project their anger onto others deny their own anger and attribute it to others involved in the situation. By doing that, they can be somewhat "righteous" when they finally react to the anger.

9. *Placating or pacifying the other person involved to prevent the loss/threat that triggered the angry feelings.*

10. *Confrontation.* Telling the others involved in the situation of one's own angry feelings and asking for a response.

11. *Negotiation with others involved in the situation to resolve it.*

The most effective reactions to angry feelings are confrontation and negotiation. Only these two reactions have the potential to resolve the situation that triggered the angry feelings. This is not to say that any of the other reactions are "bad" (except blowing up, when it endangers you and others), they just *are*. Most of the time these reactions were learned in order to survive while we were growing up.

Sometimes they may be very wise things to do, but most of the time they are ineffective. They do not resolve the situation that triggered the angry feelings.

Once we have reacted to our angry feelings, our mind and body also respond to the reaction itself. As mentioned before, some people are afraid of anger, and their fear of anger can escalate and intensify the threat/loss posed by the situation. Our bodies respond physically to angry feelings as well, and these physical feelings can be very scary if you are not familiar with them. There are as many different physical reactions to anger as there are people and triggering situations, but some common physical reactions to anger are dry mouth, pounding heart, dizziness, feeling faint, shaking, cold hands, red face, stuttering over words, not being able to talk, headache, stomache, fatigue, not being able to think clearly, not being able to move ("freezing up"), crying, or feeling a tremendous need to release pent-up energy in some way. These physical reactions, and our intellectual response to them, can also escalate and intensify our angry feelings.

After we have responded to our physical and emotional reactions to our angry feelings, they combine to create a response of some sort to the other people and the situation. This response is perceived as a new situation to the person(s) involved, and they then go through the same steps in the anger cycle. And on and on, because the situation can escalate almost indefinitely.

breaking the cycle

Knowing how the anger cycle works, you can see that there are several points at which the cycle can be broken or altered. One very important place involves the perception of the threat or unmet need. We usually zip right through this part of the cycle and don't stop to get a clear picture of what is really going on. It is extremely helpful for us to put everything on hold for a few seconds. Ask yourself if this threat/frustration is realistically based and if it is really your responsibility to begin with. Anger based on someone else's threat/frustration is very contagious. Make sure the problem is really yours to deal with!

Once a clear picture of the threat/frustration is established, you have a better chance of making an accurate power analysis. Think through what resources you have on hand to cope with the situation, and you may find that you *do* have adequate resources to meet your needs and overcome the frustration, defusing the anger cycle right here. You can also determine what sorts of resources you could add to increase your power base for responding to the initial situation.

Studying your individual anger reactions and your responses to them can be very helpful. The more you know about yourself and your body, the less likely you are to be taken by surprise by how you behave and feel. This can prevent escalation of perceived threats and angry feelings.

Finally you can learn how best to structure your overall response to the initial situation so that it can effectively resolve the problem, or at least be nonthreatening to others.

structuring your responses to anger

Ideally I'd like you to become so personally secure and confident of yourself and your abilities that nothing would threaten you at all! Since that wish is not very realistic, I'll content myself with giving you some ideas on how to structure your responses to increase their possible effectiveness for resolving situations.

Acknowledging your anger and telling the other person(s) how you feel can be very useful. The best way is to use "I" statements. "I" statements help you express your feelings and clarify what is happening. They are less threatening than statements that blame others and they are more likely to be listened to and considered. For example, if you are angry because your spouse or child was late for dinner, it would be more effective to express your anger by saying, "I really get upset when you are late for dinner and don't call. I get worried and scared that something happened to you. I also get panicky because I know the rest of the family is on a tight schedule and worry that by holding up dinner, they might be late." Chances are the other person will be less threatened by this approach than he or she would if you started screaming.

Calibrating your response to the needs of the situation is also important. It is senseless to use an atom bomb when a frown will do. It is also a waste of your overall energy and greatly risks escalating the situation. Conversely, when the situation warrants it, "pitching a fit" can be extremely effective, as I have had to learn. In short, anger is not an "all or nothing" emotion. There is a whole continuum of angry feelings ranging from slightly irritated to furious. Learning to categorize various levels of anger accurately can also help you to clarify your resources for dealing with them.

Analyzing the threat can be useful, as mentioned previously. Many times analyzing the threat shows you that the situation was caused by a difference in values, goals, upbringing, or ways of behaving or clarifies that the situation was provoked unintentionally or unknowingly. This helps clarify the personal threat/loss facing you and may end the anger cycle right there.

You can defuse the intensity of your feelings and clarify your perceptions of the situation by talking to others. This gives you feedback on how your feelings and actions are perceived, as well as validation of those feelings. You can also get much-needed support and encouragement.

Forgiving the other person means letting go of your anger and opening the way for resolution while paving the way for more effective handling of similar situations in the future. "Let's forgive and forget" is very to easy to say, but very hard to do. I've found that holding grudges never hurts anyone but me, and I decided I get enough grief from other people already—I don't need to give it to myself. I've also discovered a very interesting fact: People get back whatever they give out. People who have shafted me *always* wind up getting put down somewhere else along the line, and very often that putdown is more devastating and damaging than anything I could ever have managed. So now I sit back and say, "Don't worry, Chris. Sometime when they least expect it, they will get theirs." It always happens, because people who go around shafting others set themselves up for the same thing. Like my Dad says, "Give people like that enough rope and they'll hang themselves." I've also realized that people who are comfortable and secure in themselves have no need to go around trampling on other people's feelings. The people who purposely hurt others feel inadequate and inferior in some way. It stands to reason that inadequacy will trip them up somewhere else along the line.

If forgiving and forgetting simply is not possible for you, you might want to do what I do when I find myself in that position. I have trained myself to "turn off" my emotional investment in a person or a relationship if I can't forgive and forget. That person simply no longer "exists" for me. Turning off means training yourself to stop mulling over old hurts and slights, to stop plotting revenge, and to get on with your life. It takes a while, but it can be done.

coping with someone else's anger

Coping with someone else's anger can fall under one of two categories: either coping with someone's anger about a situation in which you played no part or coping with someone's anger that you helped to trigger. The first category usually produces anger by contagion— you're left all hot and bothered by a situation you can do nothing about. The second category can lead to escalation of the other's anger and can add to your own. There are some techniques that can be used to defuse both types of situations, however, and the following ideas may be helpful.

Affirming the other person's anger means expressing that you are aware of it and are willing to talk about it. If you don't verbally recogonize another's anger, you will usually increase its intensity. Saying something like "Yeah, I hear you. I'm not sure what I did to make you angry, but I want to know about it" can be enormously stress reducing.

Consider letting the other person know what you are feeling as a result of his or her anger. This may be hard if you feel the other has power over you, but expressing your tenseness and its impact on your preception of the situation can pave the way to negotiation and compromise.

Find out what is going on. Clarify with the other person what triggered the anger, what needs or wants were not met. Are those realistic? Is the situation your responsibility? What are the options as seen by the other person? Getting at "hidden agendas"—the unexpressed needs, wants, and expectations we all carry around for the situations and relationships we are involved with—is crucial. When all the cards are on the table, resolution is much more likely.

Working it out involves coming to grips with the cause of the problem and assessing the reality of the options you have to deal with the situation. If a behavior is the cause of the anger, new ways of behaving can be discussed and agreed upon. Talking about how similar situations will be handled in the future is also a good idea. Apologize if you are at fault, and if you can't apologize for the situation, at least say you're sorry for getting the other person upset. If, after negotiation and compromise, you still don't get anywhere, discuss bringing in a neutral third party to act as mediator. Labor unions and management do it all the time. Good mediators could be superiors and supervisors at work, clergypersons, mental health professionals, more experienced family members, or lawyers. It's best to consider these people only as a last resort. Try and resolve the situation on your own first.

a final word on anger

Anger does not go away if we ignore it, deny it exists, or fail to resolve it. It goes "underground" and makes sneak attacks on your health (in the form of physical and emotional symptoms) and other relationships (through unrealistic expectations, unmet needs, and garbled thinking and communication). Buried anger can also surface the next time another crisis comes along, itensifying the effect of that crisis on you. Harnessing anger by confronting it and resolving it can unleash a powerful source of energy for you to use (even in the "Oh, yeah? Well, I'll sure show you!" form). Some of humanity's greatest achievements have been attained and some of the greatest risks taken in the name of showing someone else he or she was wrong. Making use of anger this way can increase your personal sense of power, promote your continued growth, and facilitate improved communication with people around you.

how communication works

Effective communication demands an understanding of how the communication process works. First, we communicate not only with our words and actions but also with the tone of our voice, phrasing and types of words we use, expressions, tiny movements of our limbs or muscles, energy level, type and style of clothing and personal grooming, and with touch, taste, and smell. Researchers are continually noting more and more ways people communicate. The latest communication signals being researched are the subliminal effects of smell and odors. We may not be consciously aware of either sending or receiving these kinds of messages, but their impact on the total communication process is significant. In short, you *cannot* not communicate. Everything you do or say, or don't do or say, communicates volumes.

The old saying goes something to the effect that it takes two to communicate. One person to send the signals and another to receive them. We bring several things to communication encounters. We bring our bodies, our brains, all our values, our expectations of what is going to happen in this particular encounter, our ability to communicate, and our remembered past experiences with similar situations.

These "elements of communication" affect not only how we communicate but how we interpret other people's attempts at communication. They combine to create a series of screens or filters through which we obtain information about the situation and which we base our perceptions on. These screens are formed by values and the socialization process; expectations; needs, wants, and desires; any limits to our ability to communicate; past experiences; and our normal inclination to disregard any information that is different from what we expect or want to hear. Each of these screens or filters has different size "holes," which allow only certain bits of information to get through. The result is that we can *never* know or understand completely the true reality of any communication or situation, because our understanding of the situation is based on the much smaller amount of information that makes it through the holes in our screens. Since everyone has different "screens," *no one ever views any situation or communication attempt in exactly the same way,* even if the people involved are from the same family or have known each other for a long time.

Based on this incomplete information and our evaluation of it, we respond in some way. The other person then evaluates this new communication through his or her screens or filters, and the cycle continues. Knowing this, I am absolutely amazed that people can communicate effectively as often as they do! It is inherent in the way the communication process works that things can get confused, but there are ways to compensate for that tendency and to make our communication more understandable.

analyzing communication breakdowns

Having experienced and observed many communication breakdowns, I've found it can be useful to ask myself the following questions to help pinpoint what happened and to figure out how to resolve the situation.

1. What is similar about this situation and any others I may have experienced previously: What was going on at that time with me and the other(s) involved? Was it the same problem that triggered the communication breakdown?

2. When have I previously experienced the feelings I am experiencing now? What was going on in that situation? How did I react?

3. Does this person remind me of someone else? Many times parts of one person's personality remind us of someone else without our being aware of it. We can easily transfer our feelings and expectations of that other person onto the new person. Most of the time this is beneficial, and we transfer warm, friendly feelings. But sometimes we can carry over negative feelings that are totally unrealistic in the new situation.

4. Has anyone else acted like this toward me or treated me this way before? Who was that person? What was happening at that time? Are any parts of this new situation similar to that old one? How did I respond?

5. What am I getting out of this situation or from feeling this way? Remember, we rarely continue doing something unelss we are getting *something* out of our efforts.

6. What part did I play in the communication breakdown? How am I continuing to contribute to it? This is the hardest question to ask ourselves, because we never like to admit we could have done something wrong! But it is truly important for us accurately to assess whether we did indeed blow it!

Hopefully the answers you came up with for these six questions can give you ideas about where to go and what to do to resolve your communication breakdown. They can also teach you a great deal about yourself and how you communicate.

preventing communication breakdowns

Yes, you can prevent communication breakdowns or at least greatly reduce the likelihood of their happening. The following tips will help you increase your ability both to send and to receive effective communications. Don't try to do all of them at once. That is too stressful! Try incorporating one or two techniques into your communication style and see what happens. I'll bet you will be pleased!

1. *Remember that your actions speak louder than your words.* When confronted with words and actions that don't match each other, most people instinctively (and correctly) put more emphasis on the meaning conveyed by actions. It is nearly impossible for anyone but a trained actor to alter his or her actions adequately, because most of the things we do are outside our awareness.

2. *Intentions don't count, effects do.* You may have had the best intentions in the world, but if a communication breakdown occurred, use that as your guide. It is telling you that your intentions are not being communicated to those around you.

3. *Be positive whenever you can.* No one likes to hear bad things about himself or herself all the time, nor does anyone like to hear nothing but gripes and complaints. On the other hand, people can recognize a phony compliment five miles away. There is usually something positive you can say, but if not, don't say anything at all.

4. *It is impossible to read minds.* I don't care how long you have known someone, it is absolutely impossible for you to know what he or she is thinking, because people are constantly changing, growing, and evolving. So test *all* your assumptions verbally and recognize that any situation can be seen from as many sides as there are people involved.

5. *Be clear and specific in your communications.* You know now that you can't read minds, and now you know that other people can't either. They can't hear what you are saying in your head, so say it out loud! But remember, if the people around you are preoccupied, they may only hear half of what you say!

6. *Accept all feelings and try to understand them.* People are entitled to any and all feelings they may have. It is your responsibility to understand them and accept them as real for that particular person at that time in that situation. *No* feelings are ever crazy, stupid, or wrong. However, society does not have to accept or tolerate all *actions*, particularly those that could cause harm to others. I've found that when people know they can have all sorts of feelings, that it is okay, and that they can talk about those feelings, the need for acting out the feelings decreases dramatically.

7. *Treat your family and co-workers with the same kindness you show your friends.* We tend to be nice to everyone but the people who

are around us most of the time! I think it is high time to return to good manners and politeness. Those little conventions were established to keep people and communication running smoothly, and as such, they are great stress reducers!

8. *Try not to nag, yell, whine, or preach.* Think for a moment what you do when a friend goes off on a tirade of complaining. What did you do when your parents nagged you as a child? Chances are good you tuned out both your friends and your parents. People also soon begin to tune naggers, preachers, and whiners out as soon as they open their mouths. So when you *do* have something important to say, no one will be listening anyway. Asking questions works better.

9. *Learn to listen.* Researchers have found that most people only attend to the first few words or phrases of a sentence or communication attempt, then they focus on creating their response to what they think they have heard. So force yourself to pay attention beyond a few words and work to knock holes in your screens so that more information can come through.

10. *Avoid unfair communication and fighting techniques.* There is a way to "fight fair." Several books listed in the "Good Reads" chapter can help you learn these new techniques. Essentially the techniques are based on fair play, common sense, and courtesy. You've got all those skills, so use them!

a final word on communication

Effective communication is not difficult or tricky. It merely involves respecting those you are communicating with, understanding your own biases and shortcomings, and making an effort to express yourself in ways understandable to those around you. Following the ideas outlined in this chapter can increase your effectiveness as a communicator and interpretor. By achieving that, you can greatly reduce the potential for stress and stress overload.

how assertiveness works

Assertiveness is *not* aggression. Aggression involves demanding your own way no matter what and stepping on whomever's toes it takes to get your needs met. Assertiveness involves standing up for your rights while respecting the rights of others and negotiating and compromising to get the most needs met for everyone. People are often nonassertive because they don't believe (or know) they have rights; they don't believe (or know) they are special, unique, and important; they have been trained to believe that awful things will happen or other people will be hurt if they ask for what they want; or they want to play games, not communicate fairly, or interact honestly with others. People are aggressive because they feel inferior or inadequate in some way; they believe being aggressive is the only way to get their needs met; they don't have the skills necessary to be assertive; or they are transferring feelings about prior situations onto new situations. Assertiveness is an extension of effective communication and works essentially the same way.

your rights as a human being

The first step toward becoming more assertive involves learning what your rights are as a human being. Yes, you do have some! They are the following:

1. To judge your own behavior, thoughts, and emotions without assistance from anyone else and to accept any and all consequences and responsibilities for them.
2. To choose not to give anyone reasons or excuses to explain or justify your behavior.
3. To judge for yourself alone whether you have the responsibility to solve someone else's problem and whether you wish to do so.
4. To change your mind whenever you want to without owing anyone an explanation.

Anger, Communication, and Assertiveness

5. To make mistakes and to accept the consequences and responsibilities for them.

6. To say "I don't know" and to accept the fact that it is impossible for anyone to know everything.

7. To create your own self-esteem without relying on the goodwill and regard of others.

8. To make your own decisions, based on your needs, values, goals, priorities, resources, and situation.

9. To ask what other people's needs and wants are and then to decide if you want to fulfill them.

10. To decide you don't care about a situation or problem, without owing anyone an explanation or apology.

putting your rights to work

The rights you have as a human being carry over into all aspects of your life. If you are like most people, though, you may be more assertive in certain areas of your life than in others. Our upbringing and past experiences with assertiveness influence our degree of comfort with assertiveness in various parts of our lives, so it is important to know exactly how we feel.

Take a few minutes and think through your past experiences with, and feelings about, assertiveness. Then draw up an "assertiveness hierarchy"—on paper, with lines numbered from 1 through 10. On line 10 list a situation in which you feel very comfortable being assertive. On line 9 list a situation in which you feel slightly less comfortable being assertive, on up to number 1—the situation in which you feel least comfortable being assertive.

Assertiveness is a skill, just like many other things we do in our daily lives. The more you practice skills, the easier they become, until you no longer have to think consciously about doing them. Being assertive is very much the same. It feels weird and scary at first, but the more you practice it, the easier it gets.

The purpose of an assertiveness hierarchy is to give you some sort of framework to use in practicing assertiveness skills. The idea is to start with situation 10, apply assertiveness principles, and practice until you feel very comfortable being assertive in that situation. Once that is achieved, you can move up to situation 9, repeating the same process. Eventually you can work yourself all the way up the chart and feel comfortable being assertive in your situation 1. Why work this way instead of tackling the worst first? Because effectiveness in being assertive is a cumulative experience. Each little success adds another brick to the foundation, allowing you to feel more and more secure and comfortable. Jumping feet-first into your personally scariest situation can produce stress—and when you are already suffering from stress overload, you certainly don't need to give yourself any more!

tricks and tips

Like all skills, there are some tips, tricks, and techniques that can make assertiveness easier and more effective. Go slowly: clarifying your own values, goals, priorities, thoughts, and feelings. Consider your timing when you ask to get your needs met. Reward yourself every time you take a new step. Be as honest and as open with others as you can be. And *practice whenever you get the chance.*

After you've done all that, you might want to try experimenting with the following techniques.

1. *Try being a broken record.* One of the most important aspects of being assertive is being persistent in stating what you want, even when other people try to distract you. Don't get angry, irritated, or start screaming. Don't give reasons or explanations. Just keep saying what you want over and over, like a broken record. For example, several years ago my sister and I decided to live together in an apartment while we were going to college. After we had put a deposit on an apartment we liked, the manager of the building called me to say that the assistant manager had shown us the wrong apartment. The apartment that was available was smaller, facing a parking lot, and got little sun. My sister and I decided we did not want that apartment, so I called and asked for my money back. The manager started giving me a hard time, offering all sorts of excuses. I used the broken-record technique. In reply to each excuse or threat I said, "I don't care. I want my money

back," over and over again until he ran out of threats and excuses, and we got our money back!

2. *Try a workable compromise.* If your self-esteem or public "face" is not at stake, you might consider offering a workable compromise as a way out of the situation. Workable compromises are often accepted by others involved because they offer them a way out without losing face. For example, I decided I needed some tableware—I was tired of using plastic picnic spoons and forks. I ordered tableware through a large department store in town, and when it came, half of the forks and spoons were defective. I returned my order to the store and placed a second order. When that came, I found that the knives and salad forks were defective. I returned them and asked the sales clerk to place an order for me for the third time. She refused, saying it was too much bother. I offered the workable compromise of choosing another flatware pattern that was already in stock, and she agreed. I left the store with a complete set of silverware that wasn't defective, and the store was happy, too.

3. *Try fogging when you don't want to fight.* Fogging involves apparently agreeing with statements intended to provoke an argument. You can "agree in principle" with statements people use to criticize you. For example, if your mother says you are a lazy slob, you could reply, "Yes, Mom. I can see how some people might think I'm a lazy slob." That is guaranteed to take the wind out of her sails! Or you can "agree with any possible truth" in her statement. You could say, "I can see how you might think I'm lazy. Some days all I want to do is sleep." Or you can agree with "any truth contained in the statement." You could say, "That's one thing about me for sure. I like to take the lazy way out." All these responses defuse the situation and render the criticizer speechless!

4. *Try negative assertion.* Many times criticism is based on different values, goals, or priorities. We don't stop to think that such things won't be altered or changed no matter what we say or do, and we start screaming anyway. Negative assertion involves assertively accepting the fact that you made an error while avoiding an argument.

When someone is being unduly hostile, your best bet is to admit you made a mistake, but to camp it up a bit so that his or her hostility comes across as being out of line. For example, if you forgot to pay the rent and your rommate is being hostile, you could say, "Oh my god!!! You mean I forgot to pay the rent?? What a stupid idiot I am!!! I'll run down and pay it right now!" If the person is giving you valid criticism, you could say, "Yeah, you're right, I blew it. Sorry."

5. *Try negative inquiry.* Negative inquiry is a nondefensive response that prompts the criticizer to make further critical statements, but in the process to clarify his or her values and expectations. Returning to the situation of your mother referring to you as a lazy slob, you could say, "I don't understand. What is it about me that makes you say that?" After each response, request further clarification. Eventually the criticizer will realize the absurdity of his or her criticisms, and you will have avoided a fight.

6. *Provide free information and practice self-disclosure.* Assertiveness not only involves stating your opinions and needs, it also means being an active participant in the communication process and facilitating communications from others. One way to keep conversation going is to provide "free information"—revealing feelings, your interests, and things about yourself in the course of a conversation. Following up on free information provided by others increases their participation in the conversation. Self-disclosure involves revealing information about yourself and your interests in response to direct questions.

a final word on assertiveness

Assertiveness is not all take and no give. Assertiveness involves being an active listener, doing your part to keep communication flowing smoothly, and helping others to express themselves—as well as standing up for your rights, needs, and wants. Since stress symptoms can be produced by keeping strong feelings inside and not getting needs met, practicing assertiveness in our daily lives may be one very good way to reduce stress overload. Try it. It really works!

6

coping with
the effects of stress

We've talked about all the things that don't work in reducing stress. What about things that do work? This section will cover a wide variety of techniques and tricks that are helpful in coping with the effects of stress. Effects of stress are the emotions, feelings, and physical symptoms mentioned earlier in this book that are signs of stress overload. The coping techniques offered here can help you control your symptoms while you work on solving the problems causing stress in the first place. As such, they are a means to an end, not an end in themselves. They can provide you with "breathing room" so that you can start afresh.

These coping techniques will *not* reduce stress for you. The remaining chapters of this book will provide concrete ways for you to do that. But in order to tackle those areas, you've got to have energy. These coping techniques will help you free up some of your energy.

A few words of warning first.

1. *Not all coping techniques work equally well for all people.* It's up to you to experiment with a selection of the techniques offered here to come up with a "coping package" that works best for you. As your life situation changes and the sources of your stress change, you may need to alter your personal "coping package" to meet these new demands.

2. *Check with your physician before you make any drastic changes in your life-style through exercise or diet. Go slowly!* Progress won't be made overnight, but it *will* come.

3. *If you have any physical problem or injury, check with your physician before you do any relaxation or fitness-oriented exercise.* The operating rule is "First do no harm!" You don't need to add to your stress level by injuring your back or knee.

4. *It's better to practice a few coping techniques consistently than a lot of coping techniques sporadically.* Our bodies respond best to habit, so make your coping technqiues an integral part of your daily life. They have a preventative value as well as a restorative value.

5. *Go slowly!* Don't try to do everything all at once.

6. *If you find yourself getting in over your head emotionally, talk to friends, family, or co-workers.* You might want to consider talking with a mental health professional as well.

7. *Let the important people in your life know you are trying new ways to cope with your symptoms and feelings.* They're more likely to be supportive and tolerant if they know what is going on.

8. *Do not discontinue any medication or treatment regimen prescribed by your physician without checking with him or her first!* These coping techniques will help you feel better, but do not stop anything your physician may have told you to do unless you get his or her approval first.

Understood? Okay, prepare to relax!

breathing exercises

How often have you heard people say, "If you want to calm down, just take three deep breaths?" They were telling you the truth! By taking deep breaths, you relax the muscles in your chest and stomach and slightly increase the carbon dioxide level in your blood, which has a tranquilizing effect. The following exercises can work wonderfully, but remember, the idea is not to force your breathing but rather to relax and enjoy the experience. If you begin to feel dizzy or hyperventilated, just stop for a minute and rest.

exercise one

Inhale deeply through your nose, trying to take the air all the way down to your stomach. Most people only breathe with the top part of their lungs when they take short breaths. We rarely use our lungs to their full capacity. Expand your stomach so that you can fill your lungs completely. Exhale slowly through your mouth, trying to empty your lungs completely. As you exhale, your stomach should contract (some people do just the reverse). Relax, and repeat as often as you feel comfortable until you begin to feel calm.

exercise two

Inhale slowly through your nose to the count of three. Hold your breath to the count of three, then exhale slowly to the count of three. Repeat this pattern for several minutes. Experiment a little. Some people find that a count of four or five works better. It's fun to do this exercise while you are walking or running, timing your breathing to your steps. Keep this a smooth, flowing process and you'll probably find yourself walking more slowly and enjoying the view!

exercise three

Breathing can also help you feel sleepy when you have insomnia. Researchers found that when a person sleeps, carbon dioxide levels in the blood are higher than when he or she is awake. Increasing the carbon dioxide level in your blood slightly can help you feel drowsy. Follow these simple steps:

1. Settle into a comfortable position. If your pillow is high enough to keep your head tilted backward a little, it will help relax the muscles in your throat and mouth.

2. Gently close your eyes.

3. Breathe in deeply, filling your lungs and expanding your chest. Breathe out, drawing in your stomach to exhale as much as possible. Repeat two more times.

4. Next hold your breath for as long as you comfortably can. This increases the carbon dioxide level in your blood. When you feel you want to breathe again, repeat the process outlined above. It is important not to take any more than three deep breaths in any part of this exercise in order to keep the carbon dioxide level just right. You can repeat this process as often as it takes you to feel sleepy. Some people only need to repeat the process a few times, others may need longer.

visualization

Visualization is a fancy term for learning how to use your imagination to help you relax. It can be helpful if your mind keeps working overtime, bringing up worries and problems you'd rather not think about. Visualization can also help you block out unwanted thoughts when you would rather concentrate on a task. Settle back into a comfortable position, relax any muscles that feel tense, and try one of the following exercises.

exercise one

If a thought or problem keeps popping into your head, try saying no out loud each time you think of it. Practice this self-command repeatedly over a five- or ten-minute period while remaining in a comfortable position. When the thoughts seem to be occurring less frequently, switch over to a silent no when the thought occurs. Eventually you won't even have to do that.

exercise two

Imagine a pleasant scene, such as a sky with big white, fluffy clouds; waves on an ocean; a fresh green forest; or whatever appeals to you as a relaxing, pleasant picture. Focus on this scene to block out unpleasant thoughts. Picture yourself in the scene, what you would be doing, what you would be feeling, and so on. When you find that you have succeeded in blocking out unwanted thoughts, gradually let this scene fade away, focusing on the relaxed feeling it has left behind.

exercise three

Let a black or gray "nothingness" appear before your closed eyes, on the "movie screen" inside your head. Gradually let patches of blue drift into the gray area on the "movie screen." As patches of blue come into your field of vision, hold on to the feeling that lets the blue appear.

visualization helpers

Some people may have trouble picturing scenes, grayness, or fluffy clouds when they first try visualizing. This sort of mind stretching takes practice! If you have trouble visualizing pictures, you might want to consider using "audio cues."

"Audio cues" involve using sounds to trigger your imagination and to help block out thoughts or worries. Some people enjoy listening to their favorite music while letting their minds wander and relax. Other people prefer to use "white noise" (any steady, low noise) from a fan, air conditioner, furnace, humidifier, and so forth to block out or mask outside noises. That's why some people can easily fall asleep listening to the whirring of a fan in the summer.

A considerable amount of research is being done in the area of "psychoacoustics"—the use of sounds to create a positive, relaxing atmosphere that can have an impact on feelings and emotions. Syntonic Research, Inc., based in New York, has produced an array of recordings on both albums and cassettes called the *Environments* series (TM). *Environments* produce specific psychological effects. Naturally occurring sounds are recorded and then altered or amplified just enough to make the sounds seem incredibly real when played back on a cassette player or stereo. I've used the *Environments* cassettes with great success in workshops and seminars, and found the only side effect to be that at least two people fall asleep listening to them every time! I use them myself to mask background noise (I live in a noisy apartment building) when I'm trying to sleep, study, or concentrate, and to facilitate visualization. They are like having a safe, effective tranquilizer as close as a tape player or stereo.

There are eight albums and five cassettes in the *Environments* series, ranging from recordings of waves splashing on a shore to the sound of rain dripping off pine needles. Many music stores will special-order the tapes or albums for you, or you can order them directly from Syntonic Research. For more information, write to:

Syntonic Research, Inc.
175 Fifth Avenue
New York, NY 10010

A useful way to practice visualization is to take a "quick vacation" using the *Environments* recordings, your favorite music, or simply picturing a place you particularly like. Turn on the recording of your choice, set a timer for twenty to thirty minutes, settle into a comfortable position, and close your eyes. Focus at first on the sounds you hear from the recording or picture your ideal vacation spot. Increase the vividness of your visualization of your "vacation spot" by focusing on the answers to the following questions:

1. Open your eyes in your "vacation spot" and look around. What colors do you see in front of you? What shapes can you see?
2. Is it dark or light where you are? Can you see shadows?
3. What is the temperature of your "vacation spot"? Is it warm or cold? Can you feel the warmth or coolness against your skin?

4. Can you feel the wind or a breeze against your skin?
5. What sounds can you hear in your "vacation spot"? Where are they coming from?
6. What does the ground feel like under your feet?
7. What textures can you feel against your skin?
8. Can you detect any fragrances in your "vacation spot"? Can you determine what they are?
9. Are you with someone in your "vacation spot"? Who is it?
10. What are you doing? Can you feel your body moving?
11. What are your feelings in this happy "vacation spot"?
12. Concentrate on what being completely relaxed feels like for you. Can you feel tension anywhere in your body? If you do, consciously relax those tense muscles. This is the good, relaxed feeling you want to bring with you when you leave your "vacation spot."
13. When the recording ends or the timer rings, gradually bring yourself back into the room, gently increasing your awareness of your surroundings. When you're ready, open your eyes and look around, still keeping that happy, relaxed feeling with you. Stretch if you feel like it, or yawn, and enjoy feeling more relaxed than you've ever been in your life!

This sort of vivid visualization gets easier the more you practice it, so don't worry if you couldn't picture everything about your "vacation spot" the first time. Most people find that twenty to thirty minutes is a good length of time to spend visualizing and feel very refreshed and relaxed when thirty minutes is up. As you relax more and more, you may notice your breathing slowing down, muscle tension slipping away, and pulse rate slowing. This is all for the good. They are signs your body is benefitting from relaxation.

Visualizing can help you not only physiologically but psychologically as well. Focusing your attention on the minute details of your vacation spots helps block out worries and concerns that might be stressful and disturbing, giving you a "breathing space" and a chance to regroup your energies. For this reason visualization is helpful if you are having difficulty sleeping because you can't "turn off" your thoughts. As you become more skilled at visualization, you may not even hear the record or tape end—you'll already be asleep!

Visualization is also helpful for your body, even for time periods of less than twenty minutes. If you are feeling pressured, take a trip to the Caribbean for a few minutes! Give your mind a break! My favorite times to practice visualization are while riding on a bus or plane, when listening to boring lectures, any time I get put on "hold" while I'm on the phone, when I can't sleep, and when I go to the dentist (*especially* when I go to the dentist!). Experiment and see when you could benefit from a free vacation!

behavioral rehearsal

Behavioral rehearsal is just that—rehearsing a series of thoughts and actions you can use to cope with stressful situations before they happen. Not only does this sharpen your awareness of what stress feels like for you in certain situations, but it helps train you to plan and make use of self-instruction, creative thinking, and alternative coping methods.

Many people find it helpful to practice new behaviors with a friend, but you can also do it by yourself. I've found that you reap the most benefits from behavioral rehearsal if you practice a new behavior several times before putting it into practice.

Rehearsals are simple tools, but they require that you carefully think through situations that are particularly stressful for you. Remember, we usually imagine situations that are much worse than anything likely to happen in reality. The following guidelines can help make behavioral rehearsals work for you.

1. Become aware of what thoughts and feelings occur to you in a particular stressful situation that bothers you. Ask yourself, "What thoughts or feelings tell me stress is near?"

2. Sort through ideas and beliefs that can make you more upset and tense. Ask yourself, "What thoughts do I have about this situation that make me even more upset?"

3. Think about what you can do to prepare for the stressful situation. Ask yourself, "What can I do to change the situation?" (There's almost always *something* you can do to make the situation less stressful.)

4. Now imagine yourself successfully handling the stressful situation. Picture what your thoughts and actions would be.

5. Focus on how you will feel once you've handled the stressful situation successfully. Ask yourself, "How will I feel? What have I learned about myself and stress?"

6. Think about what you could do to reward yourself after you have handled the stressful situation. It is *very important to reward yourself* when you have done something that ordinarily would be very upsetting or stressful for you do to. Ask yourself, "What can I do afterward to give myself a pat on the back and make myself feel good about what I've accomplished?"

Most people find that it is most effective to tackle one stressful situation at a time when they are practicing behavioral rehearsal. Remember, nothing succeeds like success!

Don't worry if you are unable to reduce your anxiety and tension level right away. Remember that you have been experiencing these familiar reactions for a long time, and they have almost become habits. As with all habits, you may lapse back into your old reactions after you think you've solved the problem. This is normal and is to be expected. Just decide to practice behavioral rehearsal again the next time you know you will encounter the stressful situation. You might want to try some alternative coping techniques listed in this book as well.

Try to avoid a sense of failure, and you can do that by not setting unrealistic goals for yourself. It's also important to reward yourself when you do succeed in mastering a formerly stressful situation! As adults we're taught that we shouldn't need rewards for things we "should be doing anyway." Nuts to that! When you do something as great as mastering a stressful situation without feeling your old familiar stress reactions, you've done a big piece of work! And you deserve a reward! Remember that rewards work best when they are something you really want, not something you think you *should* want.

self-massage

Massage is an ancient tension reliever. When muscles get all knotted up from stress, massaging them helps bring blood back into the sore muscles, breaking down biochemicals that cause cramping. Some people think that the best kind of massage is the kind someone else gives them, but sometimes no one is around to do that! If that's the case, you can "do it yourself" and reap similar benefits.

When you're under stress, you might notice that particular muscle groups become tight and sore again and again. Those sore areas are your weak spots—groups of muscles you tense up almost automatically when you are in a stressful situation. Following are some quick ways to ease the soreness in those spots yourself.

head

Using the index and middle fingers of your hands, massage your scalp using deep pressure for about five seconds. Gradually work your way around your whole head. Move your hands behind your head and place your index and middle fingers of both hands in the slight indentation at the center of the top of your neck, just below the base of your skull. Apply moderate pressure here for a few seconds, moving your fingers in a circular motion.

Now move your hands away from each other along the base of your skull about an inch or two and pause there to apply moderate pressure in a circular motion. Once again move your fingers an inch or two more to the point where the base of your skull is adjacent to your ears. Pause for a few seconds and apply pressure here as well.

neck

There is a large muscle that runs along each side of your neck from the base of your skull to your shoulders. Place the fingers of each hand on these muscles and knead them thoroughly for a few seconds. Move your fingers slowly down the muscle to your shoulders, kneading as you go.

shoulders

Most people have a tender spot slightly to the rear of each shoulder, about halfway between the base of the neck and the edge of the shoulder. Find this spot by pressing gently along your shoulder and then applying moderate pressure on the tender spot for a few seconds. Repeat a few times on both shoulders.

Gently grasp the big muscle that runs along the top of your shoulder (the trapezius muscle) and gently knead all along the top of your shoulders. You may feel some bumps or knots—those are the parts of the muscle that are tensed up. Continue kneading until you feel the lumps or knots ease away and any pain subsides.

upper back

Yes, you can massage your own back! It will take some stretching, but it is really worth the effort. Reach your left hand over your right shoulder as far down the right side of your spine as your arm can comfortably reach. Using your index, middle, and third fingers, apply pressure up your spine. Repeat this using your right hand over your left shoulder.

face

Face massages are great for relieving tension and sinus headaches, as well as for providing a healthy glow. Facial massages are best done lying down with your eyes closed. Put both hands gently over your face and start by gently massaging your forehead with your fingers in a slow, circular motion. Be very gentle—facial tissue is fragile. Slide your hands down a bit and gently repeat the circular motion over your eyelids and eye sockets. Place your fingertips at the corners of your mouth and, stroking gently in an upward motion, massage your cheeks all the way up to your temples.

If you have a sinus headache, you may notice pressure under your eyes, along your cheekbones, and above your eyes. Massaging your cheekbones and jaw area using a circular motion with your fingertips might help relieve some of this pressure. Feel gently in your eye socket near the corner of your eye close to your nose and see if you can find a tender spot. Apply gentle pressure there for a few seconds, and some of the pain may be relieved. It also helps to use firm, stroking movements downward from your forehead to your ears.

feet

Your feet are probably the hardest-working part of your body—and the most often ignored. As a result, you can easily get sore feet! Here are some ways to relieve the pain:

Sit comfortably with your left leg crossed over your right leg. Grasping your left foot, use your knuckles to massage the sole of your foot. Press firmly, moving in small circles. Go slowly and apply moderate pressure. Tender spots may mean that area needs more attention.

Now move to the top of your foot. Using the tips of your thumb, cover the top of your foot from the toes to the ankle, massaging in a firm, gentle, circular motion.

You will notice long tendons that run along the top of your feet from the base of the ankle to each toe. Press firmly with the top of your thumb in the valleys between these tendons and run your thumb down the tendon to the toe.

Massage the bottom edge of your heel with fingertips and thumb. You can apply firm pressure here.

Repeat these processes for your other foot.

meditation

Meditation is really very simple—all it involves is a conscious clearing of your mind, silencing all the thoughts and conversations we constantly carry on with ourselves. These conversations can be a source of stress as we worry about a problem, scold ourselves, or think about upcoming events. You can give yourself "breathing room" by becoming aware of these conversations and learning to silence them.

Most researchers find that about twenty minutes is necessary to reap the full benefits of meditation. When you are learning how to meditate, it can be helpful to set aside two twenty-minute periods each day to familiarize yourself with how your body reacts to relaxation. The following guidelines explain the meditation process in a nutshell.

1. Find a quiet place where you can be by yourself and avoid interruptions.

2. Set a timer or alarm clock for twenty minutes, so that you don't have to worry about keeping track of time.

3. Loosen any clothing that is tight or uncomfortable.

4. Sit in a comfortable position, or lie down on the floor, a couch, or a bed, placing a pillow or cushion under your head.

5. Close your eyes and try to concentrate on something that is pleasing to you. You will probably find that your brain is very capable of focusing on a relaxing thought and still carrying on a conversation about something else, or you may find that your brain is focusing on your breathing or how your arm feels. Don't worry, just gently push that thought out of your mind, telling yourself that you will deal with it later. Return to your relaxing thought. As you become more practiced in meditation, you will find that mind wandering disappears.

6. Gradually you will feel relaxed, calm, and refreshed. When the alarm or timer sounds, open your eyes and slowly bring yourself back into your surroundings. Don't jump up right away and plunge back into your work! Stretch a little, yawn if you feel like it, and give yourself a pat on the back for taking such good care of yourself! Don't worry if you don't notice tremendous results right away. Relaxation will come the more you practice meditation.

Many people report that their powers of concentration are greatly enhanced when they meditate. Other people find that meditation sessions allow them to think creatively about problems they are facing—their mind wanderings actually turn up solutions to their problems. So all mind wanderings aren't bad, they're only harmful if they make you uptight and tense when you want to relax!

diet

When you are under stress, it is important to take a good look at your diet, because what you are eating or not eating can affect your overall level of health. B vitamins, which have been found to play a role in maintaining good health under stress, are not present in significant amounts in highly processed foods and foods made exclusively from white flour. Processed foods contain high levels of salt, and when additional salt is added to food during cooking or at the table, an average American gets 12 grams of salt each day. High levels of salt significantly increase blood pressure, and when combined with increases in blood pressure caused by stress biochemicals, there is a chance for serious side effects, such as strokes and kidney damage. Stress biochemicals also facilitate conversion of saturated fats in your diet to fats that clog up arteries and veins. Cholesterol, common in the typical American diet, has been linked to cardiovascular disease and heart attacks—also common side effects of high levels of stress. Refined sugars present in our daily diet increase triglyceride levels in the blood, raising the risk of cardiovascular disease. They provide quick energy, but fast drops in blood sugar levels cause fatigue, not to mention tooth decay and extra pounds. If you think your diet is sound, take a second look. Most of us have very unhealthy diets.

A great deal of information is available on nutrition, and it can be pretty confusing. Food faddists say one thing, and physicians say another. Who should you listen to?

Actually, the "safe" area falls somewhere between the two opposing camps. It is safe to say that most of us could benefit from cutting back on salt, sugar, saturated fats, cholesterol, and refined foods. That's also easy to do if you are willing to try the following suggestions.

1. *Eat more fresh, raw fruits and vegetables.* Raw fruits and veggies have more vitamins, minerals, natural sugars and carbohydrates, and fiber than do processed fruits and vegetables. Try to get at least two servings of raw fruits and vegetables each day.

2. *Steam fresh vegetables instead of using canned or frozen vegetables.* Canned vegetables loose most of their nutritive value during processing, and frozen vegetables often have salt added to them. Invest in a food steamer (usually under five dollars in most variety and discount stores) and learn to appreciate the goodness of tender-crisp vegetables.

3. *Switch to soft margarine in tubs instead of butter or margarine in sticks.* Soft margarine has less saturated fat than butter or hard margarine, and after a while the difference in taste will not be noticeable.

4. *Use polyunsaturated oils in cooking whenever possible to replace shortening or lard.* The following oils are high in polyunsaturates and do not increase your chances of cardiovascular disease as shortening and lard do: corn, safflower, vegetable, sunflower, olive, peanut, and sesame. Try to cut back on the use of these oils as well, using nonstick cookware, because they are high in calories.

5. *Eat fewer egg yolks per week to limit your cholesterol intake.* Experts say we can tolerate up to four egg yolks a week. If you use many eggs in cooking, you might want to try some of the new "egg substitute" products available to replace eggs you normally use.

6. *Cut back on luncheon meats, pork, and organ meats—while increasing your use of poultry and fish.* In these days of rising food prices, you may be doing that already! (Or if you're like me, you may have become a near vegetarian!) Poultry and fish are usually less expensive than other meats, and they are also lower in saturated fats and cholesterol.

7. *Switch to peanut butter that is low in cholesterol and does not*

contain hydrogenated fats. That kind of peanut butter is an excellent, inexpensive source of protein.

8. *Stop adding salt to food at the table and in cooking.* You may want to phase salt out gradually, giving your taste buds a chance to adjust to lower levels of salt, or switch to a salt substitute. You can get all the sodium (the major component of salt) you need from vegetables, fruits, and protein sources. There is no need to add any extra salt to your diet. I've found that eliminating salt in most recipes doesn't significantly affect the resulting product.

9. *Cut back on the amount of refined sugars used both in preparing and in serving foods, and reduce your intake of packaged or prepared foods.* An occasional Snickers bar won't do you in, unless you have a medical condition that forbids it. Most recipes I've experimented with turn out just fine with little appreciable difference in taste if you use only half as much sugar as suggested. Nondessert recipes can usually have the sugar eliminated entirely without noticeable effects. You can reduce the amount of sugar you add to coffee, tea, cereals, fruits, and so forth gradually and cut back on your daily intake of candy bars and other goodies. Prepared or packaged foods also contain high amounts of sugar, as well as being very expensive. By cutting back on these items, you'll be helping your checkbook as well as your body!

10. *Increase the amount of fiber in your diet.* Increased dietary fiber may help reduce risks of various bowel cancers and can reduce constipation—a common side effect of stress overload. Raw fruits and vegetables are good sources of fiber, as are foods made from whole-grain cereals and flours. You might want to try adding bran to your diet, either in the form of a commercial cereal or in its natural state. Bran in bulk is very inexpensive and lacks any noticeable flavor. It can be added to cookies, breads, casseroles, meat loaves, rolls, hot cereals, and so on. Go slowly in increasing your intake of fiber, especially if your present diet is lacking in it. It takes your body a while to get used to handling large amounts of fiber.

11. *Cut back on your use of whole milk and whole-milk products to reduce your fat intake.* Skim milk, evaporated low-fat milk, low-fat yogurt, low-fat cottage cheese, and reduced-fat cheese products are all better for you than their higher fat counterparts. You will also rapidly become used to minor differences in taste.

12. *Decrease your caffeine intake.* You don't need to eliminate caffeine entirely, but it will be better for you to at least cut back. Find substitutes for coffee, tea, and cola drinks. New decaffeinated teas and colas are available in some areas if you don't like herbal teas.

These minor changes in your diet can make a big difference in how your body responds to and copes with stress. They can also help reduce the amount of "fuel" added to the "fire" of the potentially dangerous physical side effects of stress. You'll probably feel better and have more useable energy, something we all need more of when we're dealing with stress! Once again, you don't have to follow all of the previously mentioned suggestions all at once. Gradually work the changes into your life-style, and they will soon become second nature to you.

a common-sense approach to vitamins and minerals

Nutrition is still a "new" science, many vitamins and minerals have not been completely researched, and new minerals are being found to be important to human health daily. There is much that is still unknown.

However, there is a great deal that is known. A major fact is that a balanced, typical American diet will supply *all* the necessary vitamins and minerals you need. Your body is even capable of synthesizing some vitamins from other materials if your diet doesn't provide them adequately. It also takes a long time for vitamin/mineral deficiencies to show up—a day or a week won't cause a deficiency. Much of what you read and hear about vitamin supplements is pure hype—most people do not need them.

It has been discovered that the B vitamins and vitamin C are used up more rapidly when people are under stress. But researchers still aren't sure *how* rapidly or *when* stress becomes severe enough to use these nutrients up. But, and this is an important but, if you eat a balanced diet, you will still probably get enough of these vitamins without needing supplements.

If you are concerned about a possible deficiency, check with your physician. He or she can run a variety of blood tests to see if you are indeed deficient. Most Americans are *not*. Exceptions are pregnant women (who need vitamins and minerals for two), people with genetically linked diseases that keep them from using vitamins and minerals properly (for example, pernicious anemia), people on prolonged antibiotic therapy, women on birth control pills, people who smoke or drink heavily, or people who have been on fasts for a long period of time. But if you are concerned, *check with your physician. Do not medicate or treat yourself.* In this area, a little knowledge can be a dangerous thing. Vitamins and minerals are *drugs*.

First, more is not necessarily better when it comes to vitamins and minerals. Some vitamins (especially vitamin A) are toxic in large quantities. Too much potassium can cause severe side effects. So go easy, especially on fat-soluble vitamins. These are stored in your body and can build up to dangerous levels.

If you aren't sure your diet is adequate in vitamins and minerals, you might feel more secure if you took a multivitamin, multimineral supplement. Check the list on pages 116 to 120 and compare the RDAs (recommended daily allowances) for each vitamin and mineral with the amounts listed on the vitamin bottle. As long as you are getting 100 percent of your RDA in the supplement, that's all you need! Any additional you *might* need you will pick up in your diet. And take only the amount of tablets specified on the bottle—unless your physician directs you to do otherwise. If you take more than one, you are just throwing your money away, and in these days of high prices, you don't need that.

Second, expensive is not necessarily better when it comes to vitamins and minerals. All vitamins and minerals are "generic." Differences in prices usually indicate fancier packaging, more advertising, and so on. You don't need to waste your money on that, either.

Some companies may use different fillers and coatings on their products (pharmaceutical companies have to use some sort of filler to hold the vitamins and minerals together into a pill, and some sort of coating to protect the vitamins and minerals from exposure to air, make them taste better, and allow them to slide down your throat easier). Sometimes people can be sensitive to something in the fillers or coatings and can develop various gastrointestinal upsets (that is, when you "burp" up that awful vitamin taste or have stomach cramps). Unless you already know what fillers and coatings you are sensitive to, you may have to experiment with different brands to find the one most tolerable for you.

Third, *never* take a supplement on an empty stomach! Many vitamins and minerals need to be combined with fats and other food by-products in order to be absorbed by your body. If you don't have something in your stomach, the supplement won't be broken down completely and will pass right out of your system. That wastes money, and you don't need to waste your money that way.

How do you choose a vitamin/mineral supplement? It's easy if you follow these simple steps:

1. Go to a reputable drug, discount, grocery, or health food store.

2. Look for products from reputable companies that make multivitamin/multimineral supplements.

3. Check the RDAs on the list on pages 116 to 120 against the amounts of the various vitamins and minerals listed on the supplement package. Check to see that you are getting at least 100 percent of the RDA for each vitamin and mineral listed on this chart.

4. Most likely you'll find several different products that fulfill the requirements from step 3. Now check the price: Take the number of capsules or tables in the bottle and divide that into the price listed on the bottle to get your cost per capsule/tablet:

$$\frac{\text{cost of bottle}}{\text{number of pills}} = \text{cost per pill}$$

5. Buy the brand that costs the least per pill. Try this particular brand for a while, and if you notice any gastrointestinal problems, you might want to switch to another company's brand. Your supplement doesn't have to be "all natural." Our bodies can use a synthetic vitamin just as easily as they can use naturally occurring vitamins. Naturally occurring vitamins are more expensive because they are more difficult to process into pills and tablets.

vitamins essential to good health

VITAMIN A Adult RDA 4,000–5,000 International Units (IUs). This fat-soluble vitamin helps increase our ability to see at night and is important in the maintenance of skin and mucous membranes in our respiratory system. *Sources:* carrots, apricots, dark green leafy veggies, milk, squash, cantaloupe, peaches, tomatoes, eggs, cheese, butter.

VITAMIN D Adult RDA 400 IUs. This fat-soluble vitamin helps our bodies make use of calcium and phosphorus, which are necessary for strong bones and teeth. *Sources:* sunlight, milk, milk products.

VITAMIN E Adult RDA 12–15 IUs. This fat-soluble vitamin protects polyunsaturated fats in cell membranes throughout the body and *may* be important in the aging process. Vitamin E has *not* been proven important in increasing fertility or potency in humans. *Sources:* corn, olive, safflower, peanut, and walnut oils; peanuts; wheat germ; spinach; asparagus; sweet potatoes.

VITAMIN K Adult RDA 50 micrograms (mcg). This fat-soluble vitamin helps maintain the normal clotting properties of your blood. *Sources:* leafy dark green veggies, egg yolks, soybean oil.

VITAMIN C Adult RDA 45 milligrams (mg); suggested RDA for people under severe stress 250–5,000 mg. This water-soluble vitamin is necessary for the formation of collagen, the backbone of all of the connective tissues in our bodies. It also helps heal burns and cuts and *may* help in combating infections. *Sources:* cabbage, oranges, grapefruit, cantaloupe, strawberries, broccoli, bananas, tomatoes, spinach, mung bean sprouts, pineapple.

VITAMIN B_1 (Thiamine) Adult RDA 1.0–1.5 mg; suggested RDA for people under severe stress 2–10 mg. This water-soluble vitamin helps our bodies change carbohydrates and proteins into energy. Because our brain and central nervous system rely on glucose for energy, B_1 is sometimes called the "morale" vitamin because it assists in the production of glucose. *Sources:* brewer's yeast, whole wheat flour, wheat germ, pinto beans, soybeans, spinach, barley, navy beans, asparagus.

VITAMIN B_2 (Riboflavin) Adult RDA 1.1–1.6 mg; suggested RDA for people under severe stress 2–10 mg. This water-soluble vitamin helps in the biochemical processes that release energy and create proteins from amino acids. *Sources:* cottage cheese, milk, yogurt, cheese, broccoli, mushrooms, squash, brewer's yeast, spinach, wheat germ.

VITAMIN B_5 (Niacin) Adult RDA 13–18 mg; suggested RDA for people under severe stress 50–5,000 mg. This water-soluble vitamin is used for energy transformations in every cell. *Sources:* tofu, soybeans, cottage cheese, mung bean sprouts, oatmeal, peanuts, peanut butter, wheat bran, eggs, potatoes, avacados.

VITAMIN B_6 (Pyridoxine) Adult RDA 2 mg. This water-soluble vitamin helps our bodies metabolize proteins, create hormones, produce red blood cells, and maintain proper functioning of nervous tissues. *Sources:* rice bran, soybeans, spinach, bananas, dried beans and lentils, whole wheat flour, broccoli, wheat germ, avacados.

VITAMIN B_{12} (Cobalamin) Adult RDA 3 mcg. This water-soluble vitamin is essential for the functioning of all cells because it is involved in the synthesis of DNA and RNA. It also maintains the cells of our nervous tissues. *Sources:* cottage cheese, milk, eggs, cheese, yogurt, whey.

FOLACIN (Actually a group of compounds in the B family)   Adult RDA 400 mcg. This water-soluble vitamin is essential in the formation of DNA and RNA and helps break down amino acids into useful materials necessary for the formation of new cells. *Sources:* dried beans and lentils, asparagus, broccoli, lettuce, spinach, sweet potatoes, cantaloupe, oranges, brewer's yeast.

PANTOTHENIC ACID   Adult RDA 1–10 mg; suggested RDA for people under severe stress 20–100 mg. This water-soluble vitamin helps our bodies metabolize food and create other vitamins. *Sources:* broccoli, soybeans, rice polishings, lentils, brewer's yeast, fresh peas, brussels sprouts, oatmeal, milk, egg yolks, cantaloupe.

BIOTIN   Adult RDA unknown. This water-soluble vitamin assists in transporting carbon dioxide and other materials for our bodies' use and helps release energy from foods. *Source:* bacteria in our intestines create it for us.

CHOLINE   Adult RDA unknown; suggested RDA for people under severe stress 100–1,000 mg. This water-soluble vitamin helps transport and break down fats in animals. It has not been proven necessary for humans except under severe stress. *Source:* our bodies can create it for us.

minerals essential to good health

CALCIUM   Adult RDA 8 mg. This mineral is necessary for the formation of bones and teeth and makes possible the transmission of nerve impulses. It also plays a role in helping blood to coagulate. *Sources:* milk, yogurt, cheeses, dark green leafy vegetables, broccoli, tofu, soybeans, hard water, mineral water.

PHOSPHORUS   Adult RDA 800 mg. This mineral is involved in all energy-creating biochemical processes in our bodies and helps our bodies absorb calcium. *Sources:* pinto beans, cottage cheese, milk, bran, wheat germ, yogurt, tofu, corn, broccoli.

MAGNESIUM   Adult RDA 300–350 mg. This mineral helps activate enzymes that make energy useable to all parts of our bodies. It also helps conduct nerve impulses, create proteins, and contract muscles. *Sources:* dried beans and lentils, wheat germ, bran, whole wheat flour, peanut butter, leafy green vegetables, apples, cantaloupe, oranges, cheese, milk.

IRON   Adult RDA 10–18 mg. This mineral is crucial in carrying oxygen to body cells. Most women need the higher level listed in the adult RDA range. *Sources:* liver, prune juice, dried beans and lentils, spinach, peaches, molasses, raisins, tofu, tomato juice, wheat germ, bran.

ZINC   Adult RDA 15 mg. This mineral is essential for the growth and repair of body tissues and cells. *Sources:* dried beans and lentils, whole wheat flour, soymeal, bran, wheat germ, milk, spinach, whole wheat cereals.

essential trace elements

IODINE, COPPER, MANGANESE, COBALT, MOLYBDENUM, SELENIUM, CHROMIUM, NICKEL, TIN, SILICON, FLUORINE, VANADIUM   These minerals are currently the "hot" area in the field of nutrition research. As equipment and measurement methods become more sophisticated and accurate, researchers are finding these trace elements to be important for animals in maintaining good health. They haven't yet been proven crucial for humans, and no RDAs have been established. They are believed to work in conjunction with each other and all the previously listed vitamins and minerals. As a result a deficiency in one element won't cause problems, but it may make other processes less efficient. These trace elements can be toxic in high levels, so look for a supplement that says it provides "trace" levels of these elements.

a few words on sodium, chlorine, and potassium

There is a great deal of controversy in the field of nutrition concerning these three minerals. All three are important in maintaining the electrolyte levels in the blood and in maintaining fluid levels in our bodies. These are rarely listed in terms of RDAs, because people get *more* than they need from naturally occurring sources in their daily diet. Most often, people get *too much* sodium and chlorine in the form of salt added to processed foods and table salt shaken onto food at mealtimes. Salt (sodium chloride) has been found to increase water retention and raise blood pressure. If anything, it is wise to *cut back* on salt consumption, rather than supplement our diet with sodium and chlorine. Also, most typical American diets are adequate in potassium, unless a person is on diuretics for high blood pressure reduction. In that special case, the fluid loss caused by the diuretics can speed the removal of potassium from the body, and supplements prescribed by a physician may be necessary. Since potassium has severe side effects at high levels, potassium therapy requires the careful control of a physician who relies on frequent blood tests to monitor potassium levels in the body.

physical fitness

It is hard to rationalize the time spent maintaining your physical fitness level when you're busy and under stress, but experts have found that by increasing your fitness level, you can effectively increase your energy level and do all sorts of good things for your body and well-being. Increasing your fitness level can lower your blood pressure, decrease fats in the blood that increase the potential for cardiovascular disease, reduce joint stiffness, control your appetite, decrease fatigue, and increase nourishment to your nerves and body tissues.

With all that going for it, physical fitness can be one of the most important ways you can cope with the effects of stress. Should you decide to increase your activity level, keep the following things in mind.

1. *You aren't too busy (tired, overworked, and so on) to exercise in some form every day.* You can be guaranteed an extra hour of useable energy for every forty-five minutes of physical activity you engage in. Activity will also help increase the quality, as well as the quantity, of your life in the long run.

2. *Fitness is not a crash program!* It took your body fifteen, twenty, or thirty years to get into the shape it is in now, and it's not going to change overnight. When you start increasing your activity level gradually, it is easier, hurts less, and is more fun—so you're likely to stick with your program longer. Many people under stress have lost touch with their bodies and natural body rhythms, and it is important for them to increase their activity level gradually so that they can become aware of their inherent rhythms, how their bodies feel when they are being used effectively, and learn to enjoy physical activity.

3. *Don't take your fitness program too seriously.* Exercise can be lots of fun, but many people, especially Type As, turn exercise into work. Forget about points, times, miles, clocks—listen to your body and "go with the flow."

4. *If exercise bores you, find some way to distract yourself.* That can mean changing where you exercise, how you exercise, what equipment you use, and so forth. Work out to music or run outside instead of on the track. It can also help if you reward yourself periodically throughout your program. Think about the things that are special rewards to you and then plot out a program to follow. At various stages during the program, build in rewards (being sure to give them to yourself!). These "goodies" can help you keep on the track, even during the "two-month blahs"—the blahs that hit about two months into a fitness program when you don't see results as fast as you'd like to and you think "What's the use? I just hurt, puff, strain, sprain, and for *what??*"

5. *Set fair expectations for yourself and your progress toward your activity goals.* Too many people poop out too early in an activity program because they expect their bodies to reach Olympic-caliber performance too soon. Remember, you only need the level of fitness that is required by your life-style and environment.

6. *No one sport does it all.* No one activity (except maybe aerobic dancing) can provide you with cardiovascular fitness, increased respiratory efficiency, muscle tone, and flexibility. It's as important to combine and experiment with different kinds of physical activity as it is to combine the proteins, carbohydrates, vitamins, and minerals we need to survive.

7. *Above all, train—don't strain!* If it hurts, your body is telling you that you are either doing it wrong, doing it too much, doing it too fast, doing it too soon, or you shouldn't be doing it at all. Some mild soreness is to be expected as you begin to use muscles you haven't used in a long time, but any other kind of pain or pain that lasts longer than a day or two is a warning signal. Listen to your body—it knows what is best for you! When it hurts, stop! If you haven't participated in activity more strenuous than throwing crumpled paper into a wastebasket for a number of years, see your physician first before you start a regular program of physical activity. It can save you a lot of grief later. Secondly, learn how to do your activity of choice properly and get the proper equipment. Too many people get hurt because they don't do that. Did you know that there is a right way and a wrong way to jog? Bet you didn't. So go buy a book or take a class.

8. *If you don't do anything else—walk.* Walking is cheap, easy (you learned how when you were a kid), safe (for most people), and a very effective aerobic exercise. So put on a pair of comfortable shoes and walk your dog or cat or check out what is going on around you. It's not wise to walk alone in most cities and towns at night, so you might consider walking to and from work, to the grocery store on Saturday (you get exercise lugging back grocery bags and you also learn to cut down on your purchases!), or take a walk on your lunch hour.

favorite passions

Leisure-time activities can be a great help in coping with the effects of stress. That's why everybody should have two or three favorite "passions"—things you love to do. Chances are good that if you are a typical stress victim, you haven't thought about hobbies or spare time in years.

But leisure time is even more important when you're trying to cope with stress in your daily life. Hobbies or "passions" can help in several ways: They can take your mind off things that are worrying you, allow you time to recharge your batteries, expand your horizons, increase your self-esteem, expose you to new ideas, and let you have fun with people you like. *Everybody* needs time away from work and worries—you are no exception! In case you haven't thought about fun since you collected baseball cards or doll clothes, here are a few suggestions.

1. *Everyone is gifted with creativity in some way, so forget about rules, other people's ideas, or what is "acceptable."* Baking bread, painting your living room, rearranging your workshop, growing plants, and so on are all creative pursuits. Experiment around and find out what suits you best, then do it in a way that suits you. That's all that matters!

2. *It is important to make your leisure time different enough from your work that you really do get a mental and physical break.* For example, if you are with people all day, your hobby might be most beneficial if you can do it off somewhere alone. If you are relatively quiet and sedentary in your daily life, your passion might be more fun if it involved other people, lots of action, and noise. If you do thinking and "head work" as a job, it might be fun to do something that doesn't involve thinking, like going to the movies or hooking a rug. Experiment, and remember that it is important to complement your activities at work with your activities at play.

3. *Your interests and passions will change as your life changes.*

If a hobby gets boring, check out why, and then look around for something else. Very few things stay with us forever, and hobbies are no exception.

4. *It is okay to make mistakes.* If your passion of choice involves a certain level of skill, such as needlepoint, tennis, or cooking, it is okay to make mistakes while you are learning. Once again, passions are more fun if you know how to do them right and have the right equipment. So go buy a book or take a class. Besides, you might meet some interesting people!

guilty pleasures

"Guilty pleasures" are great! They are those dumb (and not so dumb) things you love to do but are embarrassed to tell anyone about. Everybody has at least one or two guilty pleasures. Mine are wolfing down animal crackers (I'm supposedly the kind of person who is "adult" and eats "wisely") and dancing around my living room to swing music pretending I'm Ginger Rogers! Both are great releases when I'm under stress, and sometimes they are the only thing that will get me through a really rough time. A woman friend who has a PhD in design says her "guilty pleasure" is reading "pure trash"—romantic and Gothic novels, the trashier the better! My mother's guilty pleasure is working on crossword puzzles that come in the newspaper!

The point is that there is nothing wrong with guilty pleasures as long as you don't go overboard and spend all your time doing them. In fact, as rewards during periods of stress, they can often make life seem worth living. People under stress tend to dismiss guilty pleasures as wastes of time, when they can in reality be sanity savers. When was the last time you indulged in a guilty pleasure?

rewards

In our society we are taught that rewards are okay for kids, but adults aren't supposed to need rewards. Bunk! Rewards are important whatever your age! I also believe that rewards should be tangible and their size or value equivalent to the magnitude of the accomplishment you've achieved. Further, rewards shouldn't be useful things—like a new calculator if you are in accounting or a new typewriter if you are a writer (unless those are things you *really* want but keep putting off getting for yourself). Rewards should be things you ordinarily wouldn't get yourself or someone else wouldn't get you. For example, when I have finished writing this book, I'm going to buy myself a pair of opal earrings, something I've always wanted and never gotten. The "Puritan" in me says (even as I write this!) that opal earrings are frivolous and a waste of money. But are they really? I'm not so sure they are a waste.

I've also found that rewards can be very beneficial when you are working hard to change a behavior or a habit—such as cutting back on smoking, loosing weight, starting a fitness program, or practicing assertiveness—and *especially* when you are working on changing your life to cope more effectively with stress. All these things require work, an output of energy, and usually giving up old, comfortable ways of behaving. You deserve to be rewarded for a major decision and behavior change like that!

Rewards are also helpful when given regularly while you are integrating a major change into your life. When the going gets rough (as it usually does), you can prevent backsliding by promising yourself a reward for sticking to your plan of action. Benefits from a major life change don't appear overnight, and rewards can help keep you going when you can't see any results.

Think about things you could use as rewards for yourself. It is a good idea to come up with a list of about ten rewards that you would enjoy. Then plan to give them to yourself at intervals during your change period—every few weeks, every few pounds, every fewer packs of cigarettes, and so forth. I've found that most people experience a slump four to six weeks into any major change of life-style or behavior. Most people can maintain their initial enthusiasm for about three or four weeks when they make up their minds to change. After that, things begin to get pretty boring. If you haven't begun to see any significant results by four or five weeks, you may be ready to pack it in. If you haven't seen any major changes by six weeks, you'll probably give up. A couple of good rewards may give you the impetus you need to keep going through that slump and beyond to the magic eighth or tenth week, when results usually begin to show up. If it works, why not use it?

Also, the first two weeks of any behavior change are usually the worst. The temptation to give up is probably even stronger then than during the six- to eight-week slump. If you plan to reward yourself at the end of one week and again at the end of two weeks, you may be able to stick to your guns better.

Rewards can even be effective on a smaller scale when you do something your ordinarily dread doing, such as confronting a co-worker about something that angers you, telling your spouse when you have a need that's not being met, taking an exam, or working through all the papers on your desk. A long, hot shower, time spent reading a magazine or novel, a cup of tea or a glass of wine, or a long chat on the phone with a friend can be effective ways of giving yourself a pat on the back and saying, "Good show!"

So find out what some good rewards are for you, and *give those rewards to yourself!* You deserve them!

journals and diaries

Keeping journals and diaries probably dates back to when human beings learned how to communicate with symbols on rocks or tablets. Journals must have something going for them, or the idea wouldn't have lasted so long.

Many people think that writing thoughts and feelings in a journal or diary is useful in sorting out problem areas, values, and goals. When your mind is whirling with thoughts chasing themselves in a circle, it can be helpful to put things down on paper. Things that seem insurmountable floating around in your head often become manageable all drawn out on paper. Values become clearer as you write about things and people important to you. Your goals may begin to take shape as you explore your relationship with the world.

Some people write daily in journals, others only make entries when the spirit moves them. Some write poetry, others write only thoughts or phrases that are meaningful for them. Journals can be used to make notes about dreams, which can be extremely helpful if you have recurring dreams or nightmares and want to know what meaning that dream has for you. Some of my friends write down worries, gripes, concerns, or snappy comebacks to insults—and find that by doing so, they can stop thinking about them and fall asleep. Some writers use their diaries or journals to write down insights or ideas so they won't be forgotten.

The point is that journals and diaries can be anything you want them to be—from a special confidant to a recording of history for your grandchildren. You might be intimidated by the prospect of writing down your thoughts or feelings, but grammar, spelling, phrasing, and readability are not at all important. No one will ever read your journal or diary unless you choose to share it with them, and then, I guarantee you, they won't be grading you on punctuation or spelling! It's also easier to put your thoughts and feelings into words with more practice. This is especially helpful if you have trouble talking about your feelings. When you have difficulty thinking about what to write, you might try writing your autobiography as you remember it, for a start. Thinking back over your experiences, you will be able to get a clearer picture of who you are and how you came to be the special person you are. You will also clarify your values and feelings in the process.

Not all people like (or even want) to keep a journal. I'm one of those people—it simply doesn't appeal to me, even though I've tried it several times during my lifetime. But if you enjoy keeping a journal—go to it!

humor

I have decided that humor is *crucial* to our mental health, yes, *crucial*. When was the last time you laughed? In his book *Anatomy of an Illness*, Norman Cousins documents the positive effect laughter had on reducing pain he suffered from a severe arthritislike illness—it was even more effective than pain killers for him. Researchers exploring the uses of humor have found that making fun of life's problems and our reactions to them can help us tolerate those problems for longer periods of time. Humor can be a tension breaker, a mood lifter, a relationship mender, and a pain reliever.

I'm not talking about teasing, though. Many people confuse teasing with joking or kidding. Teasing is very different. Underlying all teasing is an element of hostility intended to pierce the receiver where he or she is most vulnerable. You know how some people are able to tune into the foible or part of your personality that will sting you the most? These people are not being funny, they are being mean. Usually these people tease others because they feel inferior or inadequate themselves, and teasing is a way they can feel superior for a while. While I pity teasers for this reason, I also feel sorry for the recipient of the teasing. Teasing can leave scars that last a lifetime, especially for children. Just ask someone who was called "the Brain," "Fatty," "Four-Eyes," or "Beanpole" when he or she was a child. I can still get angry about being called the "Brain" or "Chubby," and others will tell you that teasing made their lives miserable as a kid.

Joking or kidding for me means gentle ribbing about reactions or behaviors that are overdramatized or overblown, but only done once and then done to alleviate tension or cool down a hot situation. They are not based on sarcasm, but on a realistic outlook on the situation.

There are all kinds of humor: slapstick, puns, cartoons, limericks, burlesque, parody, satire—the list goes on and on. Experiment around and find the kind that works best for you. As your mood changes, so can the kind of humor you find enjoyable.

But once you've latched on to what makes you laugh, try and laugh at least twice a day—not just "tee-hees," but big "ho-hos," *every day*. Think of them as sanity insurance!

hugs

Virginia Satir, a family therapist and counselor, believes people need a minimum of ten hugs a day in order to survive. If people want to grow and develop, they need up to fifteen hugs a day. Children need even more. When was the last time you got a hug?

People under stress need even more hugs per day in order to function effectively—maybe as many as twenty! Hugs make you feel good because they show you someone else cares about you and likes you. They reinforce your self-esteem, they give you a breathing space and a break from stressful situations, and they allow for contact with other people. When you are under stress, you cannot get too much of a good thing! Hugs don't have to be physical all the time. They can be compliments, a kind word, a favor, encouragement, a smile, a "hello," a friendly nod in your direction—all the things we often forget to do. Hugs in our society have become connected with sex, but that is a special kind of hug. People deserve "politeness hugs," consideration, courtesy, and kind words too.

What should you do if you're not getting your full daily hug quota? Ask for them!! There is nothing wrong with that—if the askee says no, just ask someone else. But I seriously doubt you'll be refused. Most people are happy to give out hugs. You can also make it a point to give hugs. I've found that giving hugs is almost as much fun as getting them. In fact, the benefits you get *giving* two hugs equals the benefits you get *receiving* one hug! When was the last time you gave someone a hug of any kind? If your total of giving hugs is low, you might want to think of ways you could increase the number of hugs you give each day. The people around you will really appreciate it, and your stress will definitely be lower!

You can even give hugs to yourself. You can give yourself physical hugs such as a massage, a warm shower, a nap, a good meal—or "encouragement" and "consideration" hugs, by stopping to reflect on your skills and abilities, how much you've grown, what a good job you've done. This sort of hugging isn't conceited, it's healthy! By focusing on the positive, you can reassure yourself that you are special and unique!

So take a break and go give or get a hug!

7

values, goals, and decision making

values

When was the last time you thought about your values? Can't remember? You're not alone. In our society many people's lives are a collection of habits—habits acquired when a situation arose that had to be resolved. Other people only think about their values when faced with a crisis—usually a crisis that requires immediate action.

This common state of affairs can be stressful for two reasons. First, acting or living contrary to our values promotes guilt and subsequently stress. If we're not certain what our values are, we tend to feel guilty about everything or, conversely, about nothing. Most people tend to fall into the first category to some degree, probably as a result of all those "shoulds and oughts" taught to us as kids. Second, because values can be formed as rules to deal with specific situations, we may still be operating by those values, even if the original situation has changed considerably. I call this second type of value "garbage," and we all carry plenty of garbage around with us all the time. Some common pieces of garbage are the following: "The only place for women is in the home," "Children should be seen and not heard," "Always wear clean underwear," "A lady never raises her voice," "You should stay married to the same person for your entire lifetime," and on and on. This kind of value may have been very beneficial when it was first formed, but times and life-styles have changed drastically—so much so, in fact, that for some people these values may no longer be useful. By keeping values past their "usefulness expiration date" we increase our possible sources of stress by setting standards for ourselves that may be impossible to reach.

Much of the time we can alter these values and reassess their usefulness, and in the process greatly reduce our level of stress. I think it's important for all of us to "air out our values" periodically and throw away the garbage. That way treasured values don't get lost in the scuffle.

The fancy name for this process is values clarification, and it lies at the root of successful goal setting and wise decision making—two other potentially stressful areas of human life. In order to do those effectively, you need to be very clear about your values. Values clarification takes some time and thought, but it's really not hard. In fact, it can be fun! The following exercises can tell you a great deal about yourself and your values.

the place where you live

One theory is that we only keep things around us that are meaningful or useful in some way. The things you've chosen for your house, apartment, room, or condominium can be very revealing in that regard. Take a few minutes now to walk around the place where you live. What messages do the furnishings, knickknacks, clutter, messes, and so on send to you? What do they say about the person who lives there?

what do you carry with you?

Values clarification experts have found that the things you carry with you all the time can also reveal your underlying values. Chances are you wouldn't carry something around with you unless it was important for some reason. Take a few minutes to grab your briefcase, handbag, tote bag, backpack, or wallet. Pick out five things you carry with you all the time. What things did you choose? Why? What meanings do they have for you? What does that tell you about yourself?

things you like to do

Your values can also be revealed by looking at the things you enjoy doing. Make a list of fifteen things you enjoy doing. (If you can think of more, terrific! But try to come up with at least fifteen!) When you've completed your list, add in the following symbols:

- $ for every thing that costs more than five dollars to do (or one dollar if you are on a tight budget)
- A next to things you enjoy doing alone
- F next to things you enjoy doing with friends
- T next to things that require thought or planning
- S next to things that can only be done during a specific season
- H next to things you can do at home
- C next to things that require closeness or intimacy
- M next to things you would like to spend more time doing
- W next to those things your family, friends, or conscience say are a waste of time, money, or energy

When you've added the symbols to your list, take a few minutes to think about when you last enjoyed each of the things on your list. Can you remember back that far? Put a date down if you can remember one.

Now look at your completed list. Can you see any patterns? Do you have more things you like to do alone or that you like to do with friends? How many things cost money? Can you do very many things at home? Do the things you like to do require thought or planning beforehand? How many things do you want to spend more time doing?

Do any of the items on your list that have an *M* beside them also have a *W* next to them?

IF YOU HAD MANY Fs OR Cs You enjoy the company and friendship of other people and place a high value on maintaining and building those friendships.

IF YOU HAD MORE THAN FIVE $s You value the pleasures money can buy, even if you don't value money itself. It could be important for you to have a stable level of income in order to feel comfortable.

IF YOU HAD SEVERAL Ts Since many of the things you enjoy doing require planning, it may be useful to begin planning ahead so you can do more of these things. If you are very busy and have trouble planning ahead, you might want to consider developing interests that don't require planning, ones you could enjoy when you suddenly found yourself with some free time.

IF YOU HAD MORE THAN FOUR Ss You may need to develop other interests that aren't dependent upon a specific season, or consider moving to a climate that will let you enjoy these things for longer periods of time.

IF YOU HAD MORE THAN FIVE Hs If your responsibilities keep you away from home much of the time, you might want to consider setting aside blocks of time at home so you can do the things you enjoy doing there.

IF YOU HAD ANY Ms Keep these things in mind when you work through the chapter in this book on time management and organization. Build time into your day so that you can enjoy these things more often. Or examine why you're not able to spend more time doing these things now. Are other values or situations interfering?

IF YOU HAD ANY Ws Where did you get the idea these things are wastes of time? Whose voice can you hear telling you that? Why are they considered wastes of time, money, or effort? Do these reasons stand up in your current life situation? Why do you feel guilty doing them? What is causing your guilt?

If you haven't done more than five things on your list within the past week, what does this pattern tell you? Either you're not allowing yourself time to do things you enjoy doing, or they may be things you say you enjoy doing but really don't. Are they things you feel you *should* enjoy doing? Unless you resolve this conflict in some way, chances are good you'll continue feeling stress in these areas.

checking out your values

Our actions are the clearest indicators of what we value. If you invest yourself in doing something, you are probably revealing your values. What you value has a lot to do with what is stressful for you.

The following chart is a values grid. Beside the numbers on this grid, list ten things you have done in the past year. Just jot them down as you think of them. Anything goes—your hobbies, jobs, trips, and so forth. At the top of the grid are some common values. Under each value put a check in that column for each activity or pastime you listed that involved the value in some way. For example, if you listed "took an art class" as one of your activities, you would put a check by that activity in column 8 ("Self-expression"), maybe "Independence," and so on for the values involved. After you have thought through all ten activities, total the check marks in each value column. You should be able to see the relative strengths of your personal values as you compare the number of times you had a check mark in each value column.

Values

1 Love

2 Money

3 Growth or achievement

4 Recognition or reward

5 Self-esteem
6 Security
7 Independence
8 Self-expression
9 Leadership
10 Variety or thrill

Values Grid

Action	1	2	3	4	5	6	7	8	9	10
1.										
2.										
3.										
4.										
5.										
6.										
7.										
8.										
9.										
10.										
TOTALS										

what is important to you?

Now it's time to prioritize a little. Look back over your responses to the previous exercises and make a list of approximately ten things that are important to you. This list could include activities, traits, skills— anything your responses showed you were important to you.

After you have written out your list, go back over the items and try to rank them in terms of how important they are to you. Put a 1 by the value that is most important, a 2 by the second most important, and so on, until each item you listed has a number or priority. What are the three things you want most in life?

Now think of some things you've done recently that have been related to the three most important values you hold, things that moved you toward what you want out of life. Do your actions support what is important to you? How? If you're not happy with the actions you've taken, can you think of some situations that might be preventing you from getting where you want to go? Can you think of any ways of getting around those obstacles? What would they be?

setting goals

Once you've sorted out your values, it's time to look at your goals. If we have a clear path charted for our lives, we can reduce the stress we feel in our daily lives by removing potential sources of uncertainty and ambiguity. The following exercise will help you set both long- and short-term goals for yourself.

five-year wish list

Think about where you'd like to be in your life five years from now. Keep in mind your values and think in terms of job, home life, family, leisure-time activities, education, and so forth. If you could have the world be anything you like, what would your ideal life be like?

one-year wish list

Think about what you'd like to be doing with your life one year from now. Keep in mind your values and think in terms of job, home, leisure, and so on. Some aspects may duplicate your five-year dream, but that's okay.

Another aspect of setting goals is thinking carefully about what we do well and what we don't do well. It's logical that things we do well will be much less stressful for us than things we are not so good at doing.

things I do well

Think about the things you're good at. Now, this isn't blowing your own horn, it's giving yourself credit for your talents and skills! List the abilities, talents, skills, and so forth you have that make you a unique individual. Be specific!!

things I'd rather forget

List the things you're not so good at doing. We all have them, and it is important to know realistically what you aren't good at, too. When you've listed your "nontalents," look back at your one- and five-year wish lists and see if you can tell if the things you'd rather forget could keep you from achieving the life you'd like to have.

making plans and setting goals

Now comes the time to put this all together and to come up with some goals. Choose one aspect from your five-year wish list and one from your one-year wish list and complete the following:

Five-year goal: _____

Specific steps to take to get there: _____

_____

_____

_____

One-year goal: _____

Specific steps to take to get there: _____

_____

_____

_____

making wise decisions

Most people think of decisions in terms of "good and bad," "right and wrong"—with "right" or "good" decisions being those that turn out well and "bad" or "wrong" decisions being those that don't turn out as expected. In reality there are no such creatures, there are only decisions that are arrived at using a definite process and decisions that "happen." Decisions that are arrived at using a definite process are "wise decisions." The reasons they are "wise" are because the decider used a process that allowed his or her values to come into play, carefully considered alternatives and options, and planned reassessment of the decision and its effects. Wise decisions don't always follow prevailing societal norms or expectations. They are right for the decider at the time he or she makes them, given the information he or she has to work with at the time. *And that's all that matters!*

The following outline can provide a framework for you to follow to make your own "wise decisions," and it can be applied to any situation you need to make a decision about.

1. *Define exactly what the decision is that has to be made.* Is this a decision for you to make, or does that responsibility really belong to someone else? Do you really have a decision to make? (Remember that you can't make a decision unless you have two or more options to choose from. If you don't have at least two options, what you have to learn to do is how to cope with the inevitable.) When does the decision

have to be made? Whom does it involve? Why is it an important decision for you? What values does it involve for you?

2. *Write down all the alternatives you can imagine.* This sort of "brainstorming" can be extremely helpful. Jot down everything that comes into your head. Don't edit yourself—*everything* goes down on paper.

3. *Think about where you could get more information about possible alternatives.* If you were only able to come up with a few alternatives, it might be useful to think about possible sources for more information. The more information you have, the easier it is to create alternatives. Possible information sources might be friends, family members, community agencies, clergypersons, newspapers, books, magazines, and so on.

4. *Check them out!* Explore these additional sources and brainstorm again. List every new alternative as it comes into your head.

5. *Sort through your alternatives.* Once you have a completed list, you can begin to evaluate your alternatives systematically. Write down the values that would come into play for each alternative. Look to see which alternatives would let you involve the most values. Cross off the alternatives that don't fit into your personal value framework.

6. *Picture the outcomes.* For the alternatives that remain on your list, try to picture what possible outcomes could result from trying those alternatives. It helps to write these down, too.

7. *Sift for reality's sake.* Now go back over your possible outcomes and decide which ones are most likely to happen. Cross off those that most likely *won't* happen to you.

8. *What fits YOU?* Look over the remaining alternatives on your list along with their possible outcomes and determine which one(s)

would be the most comfortable for you. This (or these) is your "wise decision." If you are very happy with an alternative, but not so happy with its probable outcome, this is a clue that the decision is not a wise one for you. You might not be happy with an alternative but be thrilled with its possible outcome—but be careful, chances are that this is not a "wise decision" for you, either. Most likely you will have to choose between the "lesser of two evils." If you feel that you can live with both the alternative and the possible outcome, then that is the "wise" path for you to follow.

9. *Get to it!* Put your decision into action, and once you've made it—*stop worrying!* You have done your very best for the present. Remember, you can always change your mind! Very few decisions are ever carved in granite. You have the right to change your mind at a later date without owing anyone an explanation!

10. *Does it still work?* It is important to evaluate your decisions at specified times after you begin to get an idea about how the outcomes are shaping up. Think through whether the outcomes are what you expected, whether you are happy with them, and whether you want to leave the decision as it stands. If the decision did not turn out as you planned, go through the previously outlined process again. Did you need more information? What values actually came into play? Remember, there's no law that says you can't change your mind.

what is your lifeline like?

Every person's lifeline is different. Each line will have its own shape, ups and downs, beginnings and endings. Your lifeline can reveal a great deal about you—your values, goals, hopes, successes, and mistakes.

Your lifeline begins at birth and then continues through where you think your life is going. Think about important events in your life and mark them down on your lifeline. Mark the highs and lows as well. For each important event or series of events, list your age when it happened to you.

When you've finished sketching your lifeline, add the following symbols:

- ! where you took the greatest risk of your life
- X where you encountered an obstacle that prevented you from getting or doing what you wanted to achieve
- 0 where a critical decision was made for you by someone else
- + where you made the best decision you ever made
- − where you made the worst decision you ever made
- ? where you see an important decision coming up in the future

Consider your lifeline carefully now, complete with symbols. Can you see anything that surprises you? Do you see any patterns relating to risks and decisions? How have decisions affected the shape of your life? Did you actually make the decisions that affected your life?

Many people are surprised by two patterns that often show up in lifelines. The first is the pattern that usually follows the worst decision they ever made. Most people notice a sharp dip in their lifeline immediately after their worst decision, but then their lifeline begins to climb back up, usually going higher than where their lifeline was before they made the "bad" decision. That tells you that bad decisions often don't turn out to be so bad after all. They can often be tremendous learning experiences and can sometimes change the pattern of your life for the better. The second pattern is the sharp dip in their lifeline most people notice after a decision made for them by someone else. That tells them that other people can very rarely make "wise decisions" for someone else. Only you know what your best interests are and how best to fulfill them—so *make your own decisions! No one will ever be able to make them as "wisely" for you as you can yourself.*

taking risks

All decisions involve some level of risk, because *nothing* is ever completely certain. Alternatives and options may be more or less certain, and hence more or less risky. The *amount* of risk any decision or alternative carries will vary from person to person, depending upon the person's resources, possible gains, possible losses, and values involved. Only *you* can determine how much risk an alternative or decision holds for you. This in turn will determine in part the desirability of that option for you.

Everyone has a unique tolerance for risk. This tolerance level will vary for different parts of your life as well. For example, you may be willing to take great risks on the job, but feel very uncomfortable taking any risks that concern your spouse or family. Your tolerance for risk for any part of your life is shaped by the following seven components.

1. *The resources at your disposal to use in coping with the situation and alternatives you create.*

2. *Your socialization as a child.* This includes the "shoulds and oughts" you were taught as a child concerning taking risks. Usually women are taught *not* to take risks. We're taught to be "safe rather than sorry," while men are taught to "go for broke."

3. *Your past experiences with risk.* If your past experiences with taking risks were positive, you will be better able to tolerate higher levels of risk in new situations. If your past experiences with taking risks were negative, you may not feel comfortable taking new risks. That's okay, but it is important to know that, so you can take it into account when considering new alternatives and options.

4. *Your self-esteem.* If you feel good about yourself and your abilities, you are more likely to trust your instincts when taking risks and be willing to tolerate higher levels of risk in new situations.

5. *Your support systems.* Support systems are important because

they can help "dilute" the risk involved in a decision and any fear or "scariness" that result from taking a risk. Support systems are the friends and family members we can count on to help us through tough times while waiting to see how a decision turns out, or who can help us out if the decision doesn't turn out as we expected it would.

6. *The number of people involved in making the decision.* The more people who share responsibility for making a decision, the less risky that decision is for each person, because there is someone else to fall back upon.

7. *Responsibilities and obligations.* It stands to reason that the more responsibilities and obligations to others you have, the more careful you will have to be in making decisions. You can't take risks and feel comfortable doing so when you know that other people are depending upon you for their physical or psychological livelihood. People without families to support can be more daring than people with familial responsibilities.

Many people have problems taking risks. They get scared easily and shy away from high-risk situations. Most of the time this self-protection stance is realistic and sane, but sometimes our survival and growth may be dependent upon taking risks. In these cases people uncomfortable with taking risks lose out and end up being miserable. You can increase your tolerance of risk, though. The following suggestions may be useful to experiment with in order to increase your risk tolerance.

1. *Increase your resources.* Increase the skills, abilities, experiences, and so on you have to fall back upon.

2. *Get more practice taking risks.* The more you practice or use a behavior, the easier it becomes. It also gradually becomes less frightening. Think about the first time you ever drove a car. That was certainly scary and involved taking a risk! How did you feel? How do you feel now? You probably don't think that much about driving a car. You just do it. You can practice taking risks on a small scale every day and

gradually increase your tolerance by doing things such as initiating contact with potential friends, doing more things on your own, asking to have your needs met, and so on. All these things involve a certain amount of risk, and when you learn that taking little risks can have positive rewards, big risks seem less overwhelming.

3. *Strengthening your support system.* Talk about your feelings with friends, family members, and co-workers, letting them know what your needs for support are. Few people will turn down an honest request for support.

4. *Involve other people in the decision-making process and talk about the risk involved.* That way responsibility is shared, and individual risk decreases.

5. *Clarify your obligations and responsibilities.* Many times we feel responsible for people and things that in reality are *not* our responsibility. Can you "weed out" any of your responsibilities?

6. *Sort through your "shoulds and oughts."* Many of the "shoulds and oughts" we were taught as children were realistic *when we were children.* They may *not* be realistic for adults, living very different lives in very different times. Examine your personal "shoulds and oughts" concerning risk taking. Can you toss any of them out?

7. *Increase your self-esteem.* Give yourself a pat on the back! Most of the time we focus only on our failures or negative points. Take some time to look at your successes and good points as well. Don't tell me you don't have any—you wouldn't have gotten this far in life if you didn't have at least a few!

common decision-making mistakes

It is important to remember that how we *perceive* a situation plays a big part in the kind and number of alternatives we are able to create in order to resolve a decision. Our information about any event or situation is filtered through a series of "screens." Each screen alters, distorts, or blocks out bits of information about the actual situation. How much each screen blocks out depends upon the kind of physical sense alternations we have, the strength and clarity of the values involved in the situation for us, the type of past experiences we've had with similar situations, what kind and intensity of expectations of the event we hold, the culture and subculture that shaped our personalities and responses while we were children, and the kind of "hidden agenda" personal gratifications or needs we want to get met in the situation. All these serve to block out bits of the situation or event, so that *we never see the entire situation as it exists in reality!* There's nothing inherently *wrong* with this process, it is only human. But it can cause problems if the screens you've placed between you and the situation block out helpful information or distort your perception of the event so much that what you *think* happened bears very little resemblance to what *actually* happened.

In order to compensate for this human weakness, it is important that we make every effort possible to increase our pool of resources, information, and alternatives when making decisions. The following suggestions might help you knock larger holes in your personal "screens."

1. *Do not rely exclusively on "expert" information.* Remember, experts are human too, and they process *their* perceptions of events through the same types of screens you do. Seek out information from several sources to broaden your outlook.

2. *Be careful not to overestimate or underestimate the value of information you receive from others.* Our society has a tendency to *overestimate* advice or information given by physicians; parents; people of high rank, class, or status; the wealthy; the powerful; "experts" or "authorities"; people we respect; people who appear to "have it all together"; to name just a few. Ask yourself, "Does this person have a stake in my decision? Does he or she only know one side? What values might come into play for him or her?" In other words, take everything with a grain of salt, and when in doubt, get a second opinion. We have also been taught to *underestimate* information from the

following sources: women; children; older people; people of lower rank, class, or status; the poor; people with "limited formal education"; people in certain professions, such as the arts, "blue collar" occupations, agriculture, social work, education, homemaking, and so forth; to name just a few. Our reaction is often, "What could *they* possibly know?" Many times they know quite a lot, and chances are they may be able to add different "bits" of information to your total picture because their "screens" are different. So when you start to discount a piece of information or advice, stop first and ask yourself *why* you are discounting it.

3. *Listen to what you do not want to hear, as well as what you expect or hope to hear.* Process everything that relates to your decision. When we're faced with a decision, it is amazing how selective our hearing can be! We are perfectly capable of "tuning out" anything we don't want to know or hear about, especially if we've settled on a risky alternative. But it's important to process and consider those things you don't want to hear, because you might be able to save yourself some grief that way.

4. *Most importantly, listen to your feelings and "gut" reactions!* Your body doesn't lie! Have you ever made a decision and then gotten a stomachache or headache or even a feeling of apprehension? What outcome resulted from that decision? Was it negative or unhappy? If you've experienced something like that, you're not alone. Nearly everyone has had that happen at some time. Why did it happen? Our brains are remarkable creations. They are capable of picking up masses of information all the time through the screens we've erected. Because our *conscious* thought processes can't handle focusing on all of that data at once, much of it gets filed away at a *preconscious* or *subconscious* level. For example, your conscious thought processes are involved with reading the words on the pages of this book and making sense of them for you. If you are concentrating deeply on this book, you may not be consciously aware of anything else. However, your brain is picking up and storing information on the temperature of your room, the amount of light available, traffic sounds from outside, whether or not you are getting hungry or sleepy, the texture of your

clothes against your skin, how your chair seat feels, which muscles need to be moved, variations in air currents, and on and on. When you deal with people, your brain picks up and stores information on tone of voice, eye movements, choice of words, muscle tension, body position, and so on, without your being aware of it. Your brain stores away these "bits" of information as well. All this stored information at the preconscious level is sorted and organized, often while you're dreaming, and takes the shape of what we call intuition. Have you ever *known* something without understanding exactly how you knew it? That's your intuition at work. Intuitive thinking has been discredited by some people, and I think that is a real shame. In certain respects intuitive thinking may be more accurate than conscious thinking. Your "conscious" brain can be fooled, but your intuitive or preconscious brain cannot. So listen to those gut feelings—very rarely are they off-target.

Remember, *information is power*. Make sure you're getting full benefit from the power available to you.

8

organizing your life and your time

How often have you said, "Oh, if I could only get *organized*" or "I never have enough time"? If you're like most people, you probably made one of these statements to yourself within the past week. How did you answer it? Did you do anything about it? Chances are good that you *didn't* do anything about becoming more organized or managing your time more effectively. Most people don't, either—some because they like to gripe, others because they like to have excuses to get out of doing things they really don't want to do anyway, and some because they don't know where to start. This chapter won't be much help for people who enjoy griping, but it might help excuse makers clarify for themselves why they're making excuses. And it will definitely provide the last group of folks with sensible, time-proven means and methods with which to start. This chapter begins with an exploration of the whys and hows of organization and then moves on to time management and budgeting—a high-stress area for many people in these inflation-ridden times. I've found it's best to work through this chapter in the order it is presented. Once you've grasped the principles of organization, time management and budgeting make much more sense.

But first, it is time for me to be up-front about the major bias you'll encounter in this chapter. I have a real ax to grind with most organization and time management experts. For years the prevailing theory has been that people need to find ways to do more and more in less and less time. All the tips, techniques, and methods have been geared toward making people "efficient." Baloney! Most people *don't* need to be able to take on more tasks. We've all got too many tasks already, which are causing stress overload. What we need are tips, techniques, and methods to help us streamline our lives so that we can spend more time doing things we enjoy doing. People suffering from stress overload rarely spend enough time "goofing off" or recharging their batteries as it is. The *last* thing they need to learn is how to pile more tasks onto an already overcrowded agenda. I believe organization and time management are more useful for helping us "free up" time and energy for "guilty pleasures" and *fun!*

I also believe there is a significant difference between efficiency and effectiveness. Any robot can be efficient, finding ways to cut corners, save seconds here and there, or use less energy. Effectiveness involves looking at values, goals, and priorities in an effort to decide the most life-enhancing and enjoyment-increasing use of our time, energy, and sanity. Efficiency rarely reduces stress, but effectiveness *always* does.

why organize?

Even if you work forty hours a week, sleep eight hours every night, and spend twenty hours a week on household tasks, you still have fifty-two hours a week left over with which to do something. Fifty-two hours is more time than you spend at work! Organization can help you arrange your life so that the majority of those fifty-two hours can be spent doing what you want to do.

Organization does not have to be done for its own sake or to meet the ideas set by TV, magazines, family members, or friends who "fib" and don't mention the dustballs under their couches. *Realistic* organization means developing an effective, flexible game plan for your time and the "activities and litter of daily living"—all those things you've got to get done in order to survive. A realistic plan helps you get survival tasks done in the shortest possible amount of time so you can "free up" time to spend on things that matter to *you*. This kind of plan can be altered or scrapped altogether whenever it no longer fits your life-style or current reality. Everyone's realistic organization game plan will be different—based on individual goals, values, idiosyncracies, and desires. But each individual game plan will be effective for the person who created it, and *that's all that matters!*

disorganized people

I've found that there are two types of people who say they are "disorganized." The first type says, "I really don't know what happened. I used to be organized, but somehow things have just sort of gotten out of hand at home (or work or wherever)." The second type says (usually with a twinge of pride), "I've *always* been disorganized." (And then they usually issue me a not-so-subtle challenge to "organize me—just try! I bet you won't succeed!") Which type are you?

The first type of person I usually don't worry too much about. With a few hints and new techniques, a little time and effort, and a moderate amount of encouragement, these folks are able to get back on top of things fairly quickly. What has happened is that their roles or responsibilities either at home or at work (or both) changed recently, and they simply haven't given themselves a chance to learn the new skills or role expectations yet. Once they figure out how their responsibilities have changed and sort out what they need to do to cope with those new expectations, they are always able to get on an even keel.

A good example is a man who took my stress management class because he said he was feeling swamped. His old organization plan wasn't working for him and he didn't know why. When we looked at his life situation closely, he discovered that his small business had recently nearly doubled in size—just at the time his father (his business partner) retired. He was single-handedly trying to manage things while the business was growing every day, something he and his father had not foreseen and so had not planned for. This man wasn't disorganized so much as in a period of transition—figuring out new roles, responsibilities, and expectations. When he realized that, he was able to reassess his expectations of himself and his staff, leading to the hiring of additional employees and the development of different systems of handling increased paperwork. By the end of the class, this man was "back on top of the business," as he put it, with a flexible game plan that could handle changes as his business grew.

The second sort of disorganized person is hard to deal with and has a deeper problem. If you continually go through the throes of organizing binges and don't succeed in organizing, there is usually an underlying "game" going on based on an unconscious theme.

What are "games"? Games are patterns of behavior or interactions with others we habitually engage in. Games always involve rewards or "goodies": We don't do *anything* unless we get *something* out of the deal. I've found that chronically disorganized folks usually play one of the following five games.

1. *The "look at me, I'm so helpless" game.* In this game the disorganized player presents himself or herself as helpless and incompetent. People usually respond by taking pity on the player and help him or her out by taking over tasks and chores—and taking care of the player. This is just what the disorganized player wants—another mommy or daddy to take care of him or her, keep the wolves away from the door, and essentially make the world all rosy and nice. The problem occurs when the "mommy" or "daddy" gets tired of taking care of the fully grown player and demands the player "shape up or else!"

2. *The "I just can't find it" game.* In this game the disorganized player uses his or her disorganization as an excuse for not doing things he or she doesn't really want to do or feels ambivalent about. They get to turn in reports late (without paying the penalty) because "I knew the information was somewhere in the files, but I didn't know exactly *where*." They can "forget" to show up at meetings, dinners, appointments, and so on because "I'm not saying I didn't get the memo (invitation, request, or whatever), I just haven't come across it yet." Players

can avoid fulfilling obligations because "I just haven't gotten around to it yet, but I promise I'll get right on it." This game gives several goodies to the player. It provides a way of avoiding unpleasant tasks and rationalizing ineffectiveness; it gives the player a method of saying no or of not deciding when he or she doesn't want to appear to be disagreeable, mean, or whatever, by saying no or making a critical decision; and it allows the player to postpone resolving questions and concerns he or she feels ambivalent about. All in all, a powerful package of goodies. Problems arise, however, and they always do, when people around the player tire of the player's game and demand action. Suddenly the player finds that he or she doesn't know how to make decisions.

3. *The "I'm above it all, really. I can't be bothered by the mundane aspects of life. I'm much too important" game.* In this game the disorganized player is on either an ego or a power trip. Either the player enjoys impressing others with the fact that he or she can function at *all* in such chaos, or the player enjoys impressing others with being able to hire or command other people to do those "mundane" things. Many times the disorganized player feels inferior in some way and uses this game to feel better about himself or herself. Men are often the worst offenders in this category, partly because they've been socialized into this type of behavior from a very early age. Their mothers kept them organized as a child, their wives keep them organized at home, and their secretaries and aides keep them organized at work. Problems arise when the mother, wife, or secretary gets tired of doing all the work with none of the credit and calls it quits. The player suddenly finds that he or she does not know the first thing about coping wtih life, because he or she never had to learn how to do so.

4. *The "I really try hard, but nothing seems to work" game.* In this game the player suffers with what I call the House and Garden Syndrome—adherence to a set of unrealistic and unattainable standards for managing home and office. He or she constantly strives to meet these goals, but always falls short somehow. The player gets "brownie points" for trying so hard, and when he or she finally gives up

trying, the player gets lots of sympathy and understanding. People tolerate the player's mess, while the player breathes a sigh of relief.

5. *The "nobody tells me how to live (or run my office, or manage my home, and so forth)" game.* In this game the player gets to act out a strong measure of defiance toward authority figures in his or her life, using a relatively safe arena to act that defiance out. Sort of the old "They can tell me what to take in school, how to do my job, and how to act in public, but by God nobody's going to tell me how to clean off my desk, manage my house, and so on" syndrome. If you don't like the player's mess, you can lump it. It's your problem and not the player's—or so the player thinks. The problem is that very often, others decide to do just that—lump it—leaving the player sputtering angrily in his or her mass of disorganization. The player gets to put up a "safe" fight with authority, but usually pays a high price to do so.

All these games provide goodies or rewards for the player. That's why they keep getting played. If the rewards are large or significant enough for the player, he or she will sabotage each and every attempt at organization in order to maintain the flow of goodies. The *only* time organization will succeed is when the problems caused by the game outweigh the goodies. At that point the disorganized player can make a conscious redecision to change his or her life-style.

If you've come to this point, you have a powerful decision to make. I don't care whether you choose to change or keep playing the game. If you're getting the goodies you want from playing disorganization games, fine. *But quit griping about it!* Chances are everyone around you is tired of hearing your moans.

If you want to make a redecision to seriously change your approach to organization, that is fine, too. What you need to do in order to achieve reorganization is to rethink your *underlying principle of organization.* What is an underlying principle of organization? It is the key rule by which you structure the rest of your organizational activities, the basis for all you do. Everyone has one, but it might take a little thought to clarify yours, because most of the time our underlying principle isn't something we consciously think about. Architect Meis

Van Der Rohe's underlying principle was "less is more." Mine is "fast and easy does it." A friend's principle is "less work for more play." My sister's is "Nobody looks in closets (under couches, behind refrigerators, and so on) anyway, so why bother?" My mother's is "Once a week, whether it needs it or not."

All these principles are cornerstones for unique, individually suited organization styles. My personal organization style builds on easy-care fabrics, furniture, and office procedures that require minimal upkeeping and don't look the worse for wear if they aren't kept up regularly. My organization procedures follow the "simpler the better" format—and I use it to govern my choices from hairstyle to filing system to the kind of laundry detergent I use. A friend calls it "Chris's no-nonsense approach."

My friend's "Less work for more play" principle carries over in translation as an acceptance of "dust and dirt as a part of life." She figures it's not going to go anywhere, so if something more interesting comes up, she goes with that, leaving the cleaning, filing, or whatever until a rainy day. Rainy days always seem to come up before things at work or at home get to be unbearable, and on those days she dispatches all the "yucky" stuff as fast as she can to get it over with quickly.

My mom's principle gets translated as a thorough once-a-week house cleaning (or once-a-month bill paying session, and so on). She works like blazes on the appointed day and, once the chore is done, forgets about it until the next appointed chore day comes around. With minimal upkeep between "appointed times," all the facets of her daily life flow smoothly along.

Three very different organization styles, but each is extremely effective for the person who created it. Other people might find such styles extremely uncomfortable. The key is to set up a principle based on your values, goals, and priorities that is sensible and comfortable for *you* as the cornerstone for your organization game plan. Still stumped? Here's a good, multipurpose underlying principle you might want to consider: "The purpose of order in life is not to meet someone else's ideals or goals, but to increase my own ease and comfort."

the next step

Once you have redecided your underlying principle of organization, or simply want to make your organization game plan work more effectively for you, what do you do next? The next, and perhaps most important, step is to *figure out where the problem lies.* Now, that sounds simplistic, but it is where most people go wrong. Unless you know exactly where the source of your organizational problem lies, it will be difficult to design an organization plan that really works.

I can hear you saying, "But I *know* what the problem is. It's my desk (or house, or kitchen, and so on and so forth). But do you know what is *causing* the problem? Chances are you don't—and that's why it could be helpful to try the following suggestions.

If an area, object, or space (for example, a desk, file system, closet, kitchen) is giving you problems—DIVIDE AND CONQUER. The key here is to break up the whole project into increasingly smaller "bits" so that the project begins to look surmountable. Just follow these steps:

1. Divide the problem area, object, or space into sections (for example, groups of bookshelves, corners of a room, and so on). Think through how you use each section and see if you can determine why each section is a problem area.

2. Make a list of improvements you think would be helpful, and what you'd need to implement those improvements (for example, more bookshelves, baskets, and so on).

3. Set appointments with yourself to (a) shop around for the needed equipment; (b) install the equipment; and (c) put the equipment into operation. Notice I said "appointments." People under stress are very busy doing all sorts of things and tend to let reorganization plans fade away because "I don't have time." *Make time!* It's a case of giving up some time in order to get back even more. You might want to make all the appointments for one day, but if that blows you away, make a series of appointments on different days to soften the blow.

Here are some words of advice gathered through personal experience.

1. Check out a variety of places for new or different things to help you get organized. My magazines and journals are stored in plastic stackable bins sold to store vegetables and fruit. Big discount stores are a treasure mine—explore the hardware, housewares, stationery, furniture, and sports departments. A friend keeps all her graphic arts supplies in a fishing tackle box she found at a discount store. All the little dividers keep her equipment separated and easy to find.

2. If you are purchasing equipment that needs to fit into a certain space, be sure you measure the area first. Then measure the equipment you've chosen *before* you bring it home to make sure it will fit. I once had to lug a steel shelving system back to the store across town on the bus (on a hot, muggy day to boot) because I "guessed" it would fit. It didn't.

3. Make sure you have the proper materials or equipment for installing the equipment you've chosen *before* you get yourself set up to install it. The brackets for the curtain rods in my apartment were nailed into the window frame courtesy of the heels on a pair of expensive dress sandals. I had neglected to see if I had a hammer. I didn't and ruined an expensive pair of shoes in the process.

4. Read the instructions that come with the equipment you plan to install *before* you put the equipment together. I have a crater in my bathroom wall that developed when some newly installed shelving collapsed as soon as I put the first perfume bottle on it. The instructions called for a special drill and screw to be used. I didn't. I figured, "This is simple enough. Why waste time reading instructions?" Don't make the same stupid mistake I did!

5. Once you've got the equipment installed, allow yourself time for a shakedown period, during which you get used to the new organizational system and alter it to fit your special needs. If, after a few weeks, the organizational system still isn't working smoothly—*junk it!*

Rethink your needs and experiment again with another system. Don't keep something around if it's not working for you. It will only add to your stress level. Give the equipment to a friend or donate it to a worthy cause. You may lose some money, but you'll save your sanity.

If a process or sequence of events (for example, getting to work late, the paper flow at work, and so forth) is the problem, become a camera. Use your mind's eye to visualize yourself going through the process that is troublesome. What steps are involved? Who else plays a part? Where does the logjam lie?

If the camera technique reveals a time problem, try *backtracking*. Backtracking involves estimating how long each segment of the procedure or process will take and then backtracking that total amount of time from the time the process needs to be completed. For example, if your organization problem involves being late for work in the morning, you would determine how long it takes you to do each task from the time you awaken until the time you arrive at work. Backtrack that total amount of time from the start of your work day to determine what time you need to get up. Backtracking can also work for determining who is holding up a paper flow problem in an office.

The aforementioned techniques can provide you with the important "inner core" for a reorganization task of any size, shape, or kind. By forcing you to clarify your values, needs, priorities, and goals, they've helped you establish the basis of what organization is all about. It's outside the scope of this book to tell you how to reorganize each closet, drawer, file cabinet, and so on you have, but you will find some excellent books that do cover these areas listed in a later chapter of this book.

managing time

The underlying principles for time management are essentially the same as those for organization in general. Similar games are played with similar problems and rewards. I've found that once you have established your basic organization principle, you can easily translate it into effective time use.

For most people effective time use involves weeding out unnecessary chores and tasks from their day and streamlining all the things they have to do as much as possible—thus freeing up more time to spend doing what they *want* to do, not what they *should* do. Notice I'm not advocating doing more and more in less and less time. That is only good for raising your blood pressure and causing nervous breakdowns.

what do you want to do?

The best way to get a handle on time is first to figure out how you're using your time right now. Try keeping a modified log over a week to see how much time you spend in each of the following categories:

- Work (at a job and at home)
- Travel (not just across the country, but around town)
- Volunteer, community, or service group activities
- Household chores
- Personal chores (eating, taking showers, getting dressed, and so on)
- Sleeping
- Being with family
- Being with friends
- Being with your spouse or "significant other"
- Learning projects or education (include study time)
- Personal relaxation and hobbies

Keep in mind that there are only 168 hours in a week!

Now look back over these categories and decide which, if any, category you'd like to have more time to spend on. There is no use saving time unless you know what you want to do with it once you've gotten it. Without a plan, that newly found time just fades away and gets spent on trivial tasks.

priorities and trade-offs

Given the fact that you've only got a limited amount of time available to work with in any given week, if you want to spend more time doing one thing, you're going to have to spend less time doing something else. Trade-offs are the name of the game here. Only *you* can determine what things you are willing to give up. Each person's trade-offs will be different—based on a unique set of goals, priorities, values, and desires. They key is sorting through what you have been doing and deciding what is important and unimportant—*to you*. Throw out what is unimportant and keep what is important. By focusing on things that are important to you, you will be able to develop a game plan for using your time that is *effective* for you, and *that's all that matters*. No "expert" can tell you what trade-offs you should make, only you can do that. It's tough, but it is also what life is all about.

beyond trade-offs

Suppose you've come to the conclusion that you want to spend more time with your family or doing fun stuff in the evening, and that means finding a way to get more done at work or at school in order to free up your evenings. You discovered that you spent a great deal of time doing tasks at work or school, and you need help deciding how to weed out important tasks from chores.

This sort of "weeding" involves two things—a daily "To Do" list and a willingness to take a few minutes to prioritize the tasks on that list.

What is a "To Do" list? A "To Do" list is simply a list, *on paper,* of all the things you have to, want to, expect to, and need to do for the day. Some people like to write one up at night for the next day before they go to bed; other people like to set aside a few minutes at the beginning or end of their work day to write their list. Experiment and see what time works best for you. I like to do mine in the evening, but a friend likes to do hers in what she calls her "quiet time"—a few minutes in the morning after breakfast before she takes off for work, when her husband isn't awake yet, the phone hasn't started ringing, and the apartment is quiet.

What goes on a "To Do" list? Everything! Every task, chore, errand, appointment, meeting, special event, and thing you want to accomplish. When you've got your list, add in the following symbols:

- *A*   for things you *absolutely* have to do
- *W*   for things you *want* to do
- *S*   for things you *should* do.
- *D*   for things you *don't necessarily* need to do, but want to do if you have time

Plan to do *all* the *A*'s and as many of the *W*s as you can during the day. Only do the *D*'s *if you have time,* and forget about doing the *S*'s. Chances are that the *S*'s and *D*'s aren't that important anyway, or they would have been *A*'s or *W*'s. I guarantee you the only things that matter are the *A*'s and *W*'s.

fitting in the A's and W's

Now that you've got your priorities set, how do you fit in the *A*'s and *W*'s? A day-by-day appointment book or calendar can be a useful place to start because it helps you visualize blocks of time. Start by blocking out spaces for any *A*'s or *W*'s that have to be done at certain times—that sets up your general "time skeleton" for the day. When your skeleton is set up, look to see if you can group any of the *A*'s or *W*'s left on your list around similar parts of your time skeleton. Similarity can be in terms of errends that could be run in the same part of town, tasks that could be done concurrently, tasks that require you to be in the same place, and so on.

Also keep in mind when your energy levels are highest, and schedule your *A*'s and *W*'s accordingly. If you are full of energy and your mind is sharpest in the morning, try to schedule tasks that require close attention during those times. Answering telephone calls or doing the laundry may not require a large output of energy, and it might be wise to schedule those sorts of tasks when your personal energy level is low.

But remember, some tasks or pleasures need to be taken care

of at specific times—such as attending a class, visiting the dentist, or watching a TV show. Be sure to take these times into account when setting up your time skeleton.

Once your time skeleton is established, you can flesh it out with the rest of your *A*'s and *W*'s. Don't be upset if you find yourself unable to get everything on your list accomplished at first. Organizing your time in this manner takes time to get used to, and I've found that people tend to "overbook" themselves at first. If an *A* or a *W* doesn't get accomplished, simply move it to your list for the next day. If several days go by and you *still* haven't taken care of the task, it is time to reassess its priority for you. Either you are procrastinating in some way, or the item isn't *really* an *A* or a *W* for you.

dealing with interruptions

Almost everyone has trouble coping with interruptions. Interruptions come in all shapes and sizes—from crying babies, cats wanting attention, neighbors wanting to borrow your vacuum cleaner, to co-workers who don't know when to stop talking. Each specific kind of interruption needs to be handled differently, but several general rules can be applied in almost all situations.

1. *Teach family, friends, and co-workers to leave you alone during specified times unless it is an emergency.* There are some tasks that just never seem to get done after an interruption, and there are bound to be certain times when you simply want to be left alone. One way to accomplish this is to set up certain times of the day as "no contact" times. Let your family, friends, or co-workers know in no uncertain terms that you will not take phone calls or answer the door during these times, unless it is an emergency—and you define what an emergency is. *Then do not answer the phone or go to the door.* Promise to return all calls and answer all notes immediately after your "no contact" times. Most people are willing to accommodate you if interruptions are handled this way. If setting up a schedule of "no contact" times doesn't appeal to you, you might want to establish signals that will let those around you know you need some time without interrup-

tions. When I lived in crowded dormitories and equally crowded apartments, my roommates and I used scarves as signals. Whenever one of us didn't want to be disturbed in order to study or just be quiet, we put on a red bandana. This was our agreed-upon signal that the rest of us would leave the bandana wearer alone until the bandana came off. Other friends used ties looped over doorknobs, closed window shades, or closed doors as similar signals. Since phone calls early in the morning or late at night constitute a particularly annoying interruption (*especially* on weekends), it is just common courtesy to refrain from calling friends before 10 A.M. or after 10 P.M. unless you've checked with your friend first.

2. *Remove the source of the interruptions.* This suggestion isn't too practical if the source of your interruptions is your child or spouse, but it works wonderfully if the telephone drives you crazy. If you can afford it, an answering machine can be a godsend. A cheaper, and equally effective, method is simply to unplug the phone. People who call you when the phone is unplugged will hear it ring, but you won't! If your phone is an older model, try removing the receiver and dialing a couple of numbers. That engages the line and keeps the telephone company from coming on with that annoying buzz to let you know your phone is off the hook. Callers will get a busy signal. Just remember to reconnect the phone when you no longer need to fend off interruptions.

3. *Rearrange your time.* Get up early before everyone else for some quiet time or stay up after everyone else has gone to bed. At work many people have found that by coming in a half hour before anyone else or staying a half hour after everyone has gone (providing the building is safe and the office door is locked), they can accomplish miracles.

4. *Nip long talkers in the bud.* Several colleagues have had a great deal of trouble getting things accomplished when long-winded people stopped by their desks to chat. One woman learned to simply say she couldn't chat just then and would make arrangements to talk

to the person at another time. A man found that moving such chats away from his desk—to the coffee room, conference room, or even the hallway—gave him a way out. He was able to leave when he had to get back to work. Another woman brought an easily readable clock from home and put it on her desk. Now when long-winded desk-side chatters pay her a visit, she can say she's got time for a five-minute chat and that is all. Both she and her visitor can keep an eye on the time, and she swears she has been able to get much more accomplished. Experiment and see if you can come up with some of your own ideas for handling long-winded desk chatters!

5. *Picture your task as a giant magnet that draws you back after each interruption.* Force yourself to return to the task at hand after each interruption. It's too easy to rationalize putting off unpleasant tasks once you've been interrupted.

6. *If all else fails, remove yourself physically.* Take your work home, to an unused office, or to the library. Go anywhere it takes to get the job done and avoid interruptions! One of my friends hides out in her closet when she needs to get work done at home!

ways to save time

Everybody always asks me how to save time, so here is a list of "hints for the harried" I've collected from students, friends, newspapers, and other books.

1. *Consolidate your chores.* Do similar tasks at the same time or do several chores at once.

2. *Use labor-saving technology.* This principle means everything from phoning instead of driving to using a laundry soap with a built-in fabric softener. Make use of all the time-savers available to you through advances in appliances, house maintenance, gardening, cleaning, and keeping an office going.

3. *Simplify your life.* This principle can be applied to everything from personal appearance to your yard and garden. Choose things for your life and home that coincide with the amount of time you have to spend on them.

4. *Draft family members to help out.* There is absolutely no reason why able-bodied family members, whatever their ages, cannot help maintain a household and keep it running efficiently, whether Mom works or not. If they get it dirty, they can help clean it up, and *do not accept excuses!*

5. *Reassess your standards.* Sift through your standards and expectations in regard to cleanliness, entertaining, cooking, landscaping, neatness, and so on. Many of our standards and expectations can be relaxed or modified without doing anyone any harm. Something has to give when you're working, going to school, and/or keeping up a home, and it's less stress inducing to let dust gather in the corners than to spend less time with your family and friends.

6. *Get the equipment you need to do the job and buy the best you can afford.* Keep this equipment in good condition and you cut your chore time in half.

And finally, and perhaps most importantly, *learn to say no!!*

managing procrastination

Everyone procrastinates, but some of us are better at it than others. People usually procrastinate when they are ambivalent about doing something, really don't want to do something, are angry about something, or feel overwhelmed or frightened by some aspect of the task. You can procrastinate by indulging yourself (in an extra cup of coffee, taking a nap, and so on), socializing, reading (either something else or more than you need to do to complete a task), doing it yourself when it can more effectively be done by someone else, overdoing it (making homemade bread from scratch when a loaf of bread from the grocery would be more than adequate, for example), running away (either mentally or physically), or daydreaming.

Some people swear they produce better under pressure, but that is usually a myth they've talked themselves into believing. When you are already under stress, your mind and body do not need additional stress from procrastination.

All experts believe the best way to deal with a bad case of procrastination is to analyze what is causing you to procrastinate. The following ideas may provide you with some new ways to tackle procrastination.

1. *Change your habits.* If you have gotten into the habit of putting off writing term papers until the last minute or not paying bills until they are overdue, for example, you've got to revamp your habits and set up new ones. Decide what sort of habits would work more effectively for you and gradually establish these new habits into your life-style. Reward yourself when you use your new habits and be understanding when you backslide into your old ones (as everyone does at some point). It's easier to institute one new habit at a time and to go slowly at first.

2. *Use the "Divide and Conquer" principle.* If you find yourself procrastinating either because a task is overwhelming or because you simply dislike it, try dividing the overall task into several smaller ones. Tasks seem to go faster that way, and each piece can be done relatively painlessly.

3. *Evaluate your "Balance Sheet."* Use a balance sheet to list the pros and cons of not doing the task at hand. Usually this technique can shape up the most hard-core procrastinator!

4. *Establish a "Job Jar."* This technique works best for those nagging, unpleasant tasks around the house or workplace most of us would rather not do. On slips of paper make notes about all those nasty tasks and put all the notes into a big jar or box. When you have free time, or on a regular weekly schedule, dip into the job jar and complete

whatever task you end up with. No fair putting notes back and fishing around to find a less disagreeable chore!

5. *If all else fails, cut off your escape routes.* Lock yourself in a room with nothing to do but the task at hand, and get to it! Promise yourself a suitable reward for finishing the unpleasant task. Or go to the library to study—where there is no refrigerator, stereo, or TV to tempt you.

managing your money

A high-stress area for most people these days is money. With high inflation and shrinking take-home pay, we could all use some no-nonsense information on how to make our dollars go farther. Developing a "spending plan" based on *your* personal goals, values, and priorities is the key. No one budget works equally well for everyone. But a "personal spending plan" does work.

Where do you start creating a "personal spending plan"? To begin wtih, you need to figure out how much money you can count on bringing home each month. Notice I said "count on." You need to know the minimum you will have to work with each month. Don't count on any extra money until you've got it. When you do get it, use it to pay more on bills, to put into a savings account, and so on.

The next step is to list your *fixed* expenses. Fixed expenses are the things you *must* pay each month. Usually you have to pay the same amount each month as well, so you can work up a "spending skeleton" that will be fairly accurate for each month. Fixed expenses can include rent or mortgage payments; day care expenses; heat, electricity, or water bills; taxes; credit card or loan installment payments; insurance premiums; medications; car payments; tuition; and anything else you must pay each month.

Next, list your *flexible* expenses. Flexible expenses are those things that could be cut back on or altered—in other words, you don't have to pay the same amount each month. Flexible expenses can include food; gasoline or public transportation costs; clothes; contributions to civic and/or church charities; furniture; entertainment;

hobbies; gifts; newspapers, books, and magazines; personal grooming aids; vacations; personal spending allowance; savings; and anything else you spend money on that you don't have to allocate a fixed amount to every month. Notice I put savings in this category. If saving is very high on your list of priorities, you may want to put it into your fixed-expenses category. But most of my students saw it as a flexible expense.

When you have completed your fixed- and flexible-expense lists, estimate a dollar value for each item on both lists. This should be easy to do for fixed expenses—you can look back through your checkbook or receipts. Dollar figures for your flexible expenses might be a little harder to estimate. Try keeping track for a week or so of where your money goes if you really cannot estimate a figure. Add up the figures for each list. Subtract your fixed-expenses total from your expected take-home pay. The amount that is left over is the amount you can safely use for flexible expenses each month.

What if your fixed expenses are more than your take-home pay? If this is the case, you may need to do some serious thinking about how to lower your fixed expenses, or consider ways to increase your take-home pay. Moving to less-expensive housing, switching to public transportation, switching jobs, moonlighting, and so on are all options you might want to consider. If you are in over your head with credit card payments, you could find credit counseling to be extremely helpful and stress reducing.

Most people find that they can cover their fixed expenses, but the amount they have left over for flexible expenses is less than they would like. If you aren't in a position to increase your take-home pay to cover this gap, trade-offs are the name of the game. Somehow your flexible expenses have to be reduced. This is where values come into play. Only you can decide which areas or items you are comfortable reducing or cutting out. Spend an evening sorting through your values for each item on your flexible-expenses list. Decide first what you are *not* willing to change, then what you would be willing to eliminate, and finally what you could cut back on. Created this way, a "personal spending plan" will fit your needs, values, goals, and priorities given your present income. You may choose to reevaluate it if your financial situation or life-style changes. It's a good idea to plan to assess the changes you've made after a month to see if things are really working out as you thought they would. If it seems that you are still having trouble making ends meet, sit down again and think through each item on your flexible-expenses list. Were your estimates inadequate? Do you need more information? Can you cut out anything else on your list? Your "personal spending plan" will be different from everyone else's, but as long as your plan is based on your needs, values, priorities, and goals, *that's all that matters!*

cutting back—things to think about

If you decided you were willing to cut back in certain areas, you might want to consider trying some of the following ideas that have worked for me or for my students, friends, and family members.

1. *Food.* Perhaps the biggest way to cut back on food expenses is to reassess your eating habits. Highly processed and convenience foods are very expensive and provide inadequate nutrition. Meat is becoming increasingly expensive, so that switching to alternative protein sources (such as fish, cheese, eggs, beans, and so on) can result in big savings. Many large grocery stores offer "generic" products, which are acceptable once you get used to minor differences in texture, color, taste, and so on. Clipping and using coupons and refunds can really pay off—as long as you don't use coupons for items you ordinarily wouldn't buy. Keep an eye out for sales. Most local newspapers have a special section each week with large ads from major grocery stores listing their specials and sales.

2. *Clothing.* If it's practical for you, sewing your own clothes can afford you a tremendous savings, especially if you can purchase material on sale. (I make all my own clothes, and believe me, the quality of the clothing is better than I can find in stores, I save tons of money, and it helps me relax.) It is also possible to get good buys at "end of season" sales. More people than ever are frequenting thrift stores, secondhand clothing shops, and yard sales to pick up quality clothing at a fraction of its original cost. (They are also good ways to get rid of unused clothing and make some extra money for yourself.) Larger

cities often have "cut label" stores, where name-brand merchandise is available at greatly reduced prices, but with the labels removed.

3. *Furniture.* Watch classified ads in newspapers for household furniture, yard sales, and auctions. A newspaper in my city has reported a 40 percent increase in classified ad use as more people are selling things they don't want rather than giving or throwing them away. (Once again, this is a good way to pick up extra cash for unused items around your house.) Check out thrift shops, secondhand furniture stores, discount outlets, and large furniture dealers for sales and reduced items.

4. *Transportation.* The biggest money saver is using public transportation (if it is available in your area) or car-pooling. Once you learn to navigate your local mass-transit system and learn to adjust your schedule to theirs, I bet you'll become a confirmed user. Many folks are purchasing cars that provide better gas mileage. If that's not feasible for you, try cutting back on the number of trips you take each week in your car—consolidate errands stock up when you go to the grocery store, and so on. These "quickie" trips really add up. Whenever possible, *walk!*

5. *Entertainment.* Many movie theaters offer reduced rates at certain times to lure patrons back to the movies. Take advantage of these specials, and bring your own popcorn. For less than 15¢ you can pop the same amount the theater charges $1.25 for. Reassess your home entertaining. In the past year all my friends have agreed to host potlucks at their homes rather than having the host family pay the entire cost. It is also lots of fun to see what other people will bring! Scale down your expectations and standards when entertaining. Jug wines can adequately replace a full bar, and gourmet meals are not mandatory. In larger cities, many plays and ballets offer reduced ticket prices at certain times. Take advantage of these if you can fit them into your schedule. If you live near a college, university, or community college, you may be able to take advantage of low-cost tickets on everything from sports events to foreign films and operas.

The list of possible ways to cut back on flexible expenses is almost endless. All it takes is some creativity! Different ways will work for different people, so experiment and see which combination works best for you!

After all is said and done, the most effective management or organization plan for your daily life, time, or money is one based on your personal values, goals, priorities, needs, and resources. Only you can create such plans. No one else can do it for you. It takes an initial investment of time and effort, but the results are really worthwhile. And remember, you can *always* alter, or even scrap entirely, any plan you create as your life-style, values, priorities, resources, or needs change.

9

the last word

Well, this is the end of the book, but hopefully only the beginning of a happier and less stressful life-style for you! If you practiced, tried, and experimented with all the ideas presented in this book and don't really feel any different yet, take heart. It takes a while to incorporate major changes such as those I've suggested into your life-style, and it may take some time before you notice any significant changes. Some people who have been under a great deal of stress without really being aware of it may actually find that things will get worse for a bit before they get better. That is only because they were not aware of the effect stress was having on them, and now that they know how stress can effect them, they see it everywhere. I promise, if you create a package of coping techniques and work on the underlying causes of your stress, your symptoms and physical effects will diminish. I wish I could say that your stress would go away completely, but that is impossible. The only time you won't experience stress is when you are dead, and we are not even sure about that yet!

What I do hope is that you will come to appreciate stress as a great growth producer, pushing you to try new things, take risks, and continue developing and evolving as a human being. Stress can be a very positive force in our lives—once we determine what our individual, unique optimal level of stress is—that level of stress that keeps us active, on our toes, and involved in life, but doesn't overwhelm us or tire us out. Harnessing the energy stress can produce will help you accomplish great things.

If you picked up this book even though you weren't experiencing very much stress or many of its symptoms, I hope you've learned how to prevent yourself from ever reaching serious stress overload levels. By taking care of your body, maintaining high levels of wellness, and expanding your self-knowledge and your "bag of tricks," you can provide yourself with the optimum conditions for your continued growth and development as a human being.

If nothing else, I hope this book brought you a few chuckles and made you think about a new idea—at least once! If I've been able to accomplish that through this book, all the hours I've spent and stress I've experienced writing this book have been worth it!!

Keep growing!!

10
good reads

There are a variety of good books available that can supplement the different chapters in this book. Many students who have taken my stress management classes found they became particularly interested in an area covered briefly during the class and enjoyed reading additional materials to supplement their knowledge in that area. The following bibliography is provided to help you easily find some "good reads" that further discuss topics covered briefly in this book. All these books are easily available in local bookstores, community news centers, and discount stores. Almost all of the books included in this list are available in paperback, and most are inexpensive.

how stress works

FORBES, R. *Life Stress.* New York: Dolphin, Doubleday, 1979.

FRIEDMAN, M. and R. ROSENMAN. *Type A Behavior and Your Heart.* Greenwich, Conn.: Fawcett Publishing, Inc., 1974.

SELIGMAN, M. E. P. *Helplessness.* San Francisco: W.H. Freeman & Company Publishers, 1975.

SELYE, H. *The Stress of Life.* Rev. ed. New York: McGraw-Hill, 1976.

SELYE, H. *Stress without Distress.* Philadelphia: Lippincott, 1974.

TANNER, O. *Stress.* New York: Time-Life Books, 1976.

stress-related problems and disorders

BERNE, E. *Sex in Human Loving.* New York: Pocket Books, 1970.

BOSTON WOMEN'S HEALTH COLLECTIVE. *Our Bodies, Ourselves.* Rev. ed. New York: Simon & Schuster, 1979.

COMFORT, A. *The Joy of Sex.* New York: Simon & Schuster, 1976.

COMFORT, A. *More Joy of Sex.* New York: Simon & Schuster, 1978.

COOKE, C. W. and S. D. WORKIN. *The Ms. Guide to Women's Health.* Garden City, N.Y.: Anchor Press, Doubleday, 1979.

DeROSIS, H. A. and V. Y. PELLEGRINO. *The Book of Hope—How Women Can Overcome Depression.* New York: Bantam, 1979.

FARQUHAR, J. W. *The American Way of Life Need Not Be Hazardous to Your Health.* New York: W. W. Norton & Co., Inc., 1978.

FUCHS, E. *The Second Season—Life, Love, and Sex for Women in the Middle Years.* Garden City, N.Y.: Anchor Press, Doubleday, 1978.

HAMILTON, R. *The Herpes Book.* Los Angeles: J. P. Tarcher Inc., 1980.

"J." *Total Loving.* New York: Pocket Books, 1979.

JULTY, S. *Men's Bodies, Men's Selves.* New York: Delta, 1979.

KERR, C. *Sex for Women—Who Want to Have Fun and Loving Relationships with Equals.* New York: Dell Pub. Co., Inc., 1979.

LAIR, J. *Sex: If I Didn't Laugh I'd Cry.* Garden City, N.Y.: Doubleday, 1979.

PELLETIER, K. R. *Mind as Healer, Mind as Slayer: A Holistic Approach to Preventing Stress Disorders.* New York: Delta, 1977.

RALEY, P. E. *Making Love: How to Be Your Own Sex Therapist.* New York: Dial Press, 1979.

REGESTEIN, Q. R. *Sound Sleep.* New York: Simon & Schuster, 1980.

REITZ, R. *Menopause: A Positive Approach.* New York: Penguin, 1977.

RUBIN, T. I. *Compassion and Self-Hate: An Alternative to Despair.* New York: Ballantine, 1975.

SAPAR, J. R. and K. R. MAGEE. *Freedom from Headaches.* New York: Simon & Schuster, 1978.

SKOGLUND, E. *Beyond Loneliness.* Garden City, N.Y.: Doubleday, 1980.

anger, communication, and assertiveness

BABCOCK, D. E. and T. D. KEEPERS. *Raising Kids OK.* New York: Avon, 1976.

BACH, G. R. and R. M. DEUTSCH. *Pairing: How to Achieve Genuine Intimacy.* New York: Avon, 1970.

BACH, G. R. and R. M. DEUTSCH. *Stop! You're Driving Me Crazy.* New York: Putnam's, 1979.

BACH, G. R. and H. GOLDBERG. *Creative Aggression.* New York: Avon, 1974.

BACH, G. R. and P. WYDEN. *The Intimate Enemy.* New York: Avon, 1968.

BAER, J. *How to be an Assertive (Not Aggressive) Woman.* New York: Signet, NAL, 1976.

BERNE, E. *Beyond Games and Scripts.* New York: Grove Press, 1976.

BLOOM, L. Z., K. COBURN, and J. PEARLMAN. *The New Assertive Woman.* New York: Dell Pub. Co., Inc., 1975.

DYER. W. W. *Pulling Your Own Strings.* New York: Avon, 1978.

HALLERT, K. *A Guide for Single Parents.* Millbrae, Calif.: Celestial Arts, 1974.

JONGEWARD, D. and D. SCOTT. *Women as Winners*. Reading, Mass.: Addison-Wesley, 1976.

MACKENZIE, R. A. *The Time Trap: How to Get More Done in Less Time*. New York: McGraw-Hill, 1972.

SCORESBY, A. L. *The Marriage Dialogue*. Reading, Mass.: Addison-Wesley, 1977.

SMITH, M. J. *When I Say No, I Feel Guilty*. New York: Bantam, 1975.

STONE, J. and J. BACHNER. *Speaking Up*. New York: McGraw-Hill, 1977.

WAHLROOS, S. *Family Communication*. New York: NAL, 1974.

coping with the effects of stress

ANDERSON, B. *Stretching*. Bolinas, Calif.: Shelter Publications, 1980.

ARDELL, D. B. *High Level Wellness*. New York: Bantam, 1979.

BENSON, H. *The Relaxation Response*. New York: Avon, 1975.

BERKLEY HOLISTIC HEALTH CENTER. *The Holistic Health Handbook*. Berkley, Calif.: And/Or Press, 1978.

BROWN, B. B. *Stress and the Art of Biofeedback*. New York: Harper & Row, Pub., 1977.

COOPER, K. H. *Aerobics for Women; The Aerobics Way; The New Aerobics*. New York: Bantam, 1975–1979.

DAVIS, J. T. *Walking!* New York: Bantam, 1979.

DYER, W. W. *Your Erroneous Zones*. New York: Avon, 1979.

FIXX, J. *The Complete Book of Running*. New York: Random House, 1979.

FIXX, J. *Second Book of Running*. New York: Random House, 1980.

GOULD, R. L. *Transformations: Growth and Change in Adult Life*. New York: Touchstone Books, 1978.

JOHNSON, S. M. *First Person Singular: Living the Good Life Alone*. New York: Signet, NAL, 1977.

LANCE, K. *Getting Strong*. New York: Bantam, 1979.

LANCE, K. *Running for Health and Beauty*. New York: Bantam, 1978.

LENZ, F. P. *Total Relaxation*. Indianapolis: Bobbs-Merrill, 1980.

MOREHOUSE, L. E. and L. GROSS. *Total Fitness in 30 Minutes a Week.* New York: Pocket Books, 1976.

SHARPE, R. and D. LEWIS. *Thrive on Stress.* New York: Warner Books, 1977.

SOBEL, D. S. and F. L. HORNBACHER. *To Your Health!* New York: Grossman Publishers, 1973.

STEINER, C. *Scripts People Live.* New York: Bantam, 1975.

SUSSMAN, S. and R. GOODE. *The Magic of Walking.* Rev. ed. New York: Fireside Books, Simon & Schuster, 1980.

VICKERY, R. *LifePlan.* Reading, Mass.: Addison-Wesley, 1980.

WANDERER, A. and T. CABOT. *Letting Go.* New York: Warner Books, 1978.

WILKIE, J. *The Divorced Woman's Handbook.* New York: Morrow, 1980.

values, goals, and decision making

BURACK, E. H., M. ALBRECHT, and H. SEITLER. *Growing: A Woman's Guide to Career Satisfaction.* Belmont, Calif.: Lifetime Learning Publications, 1980.

GOODMAN, E. *Turning Points.* New York: Fawcett Books Group—CBS Publications, 1979.

GREIFF, B. G. and P. K. HUNTER. *Tradeoffs: Executive, Family, and Organizational Life.* New York: NAL, 1980.

JANIS, I. L. and L. MANN. *Decision Making: A Psychological Analysis of Conflict, Choice, and Commitment.* New York: Free Press, 1977.

LEVINSON, D. J. *The Seasons of a Man's Life.* New York: Ballantine, 1978.

LORING, R. K. *New Life Options: The Working Woman's Resource Book.* New York: McGraw-Hill, 1978.

ROBERTSON, C. *Divorce and Decision Making—A Woman's Guide.* Chicago: Follett Publishing Company, 1980.

SCHOLTZ, N. T., J. S. PRINCE, and G. P. MILLER. *How to Decide: A Workbook for Women.* New York: Avon, 1978.

SHEEHY, G. *Passages.* New York: Bantam, 1977.

SIMON, S. *Meeting Yourself Halfway.* Niles, Ill.: Argus Communications, 1974.

VISCOTT, D. *Risking.* New York: Pocket Books, 1977.

WHEELER, D. D. and I. L. JANIS. *A Practical Guide for Making Decisions.* New York: Free Press, 1980.

WYCKOFF, H. *Solving Women's Problems—Through Awareness, Action, and Contact.* New York: Grove Press, 1977.

organizing your time and your life

BLISS, E. C. *Getting Things Done.* New York: Bantam, 1978.

CONRAN, S. *Superwoman—For Every Woman Who Hates Housework.* New York: Crown Publishers, 1978.

CURTIS, J. *A Guide for Working Mothers.* New York: Touchstone Books, Simon & Schuster, 1975.

FANNING, T. and R. FANNING. *Get It All Done and Still Be Human.* New York: Ballantine, 1979.

LAKEIN, A. *How to Get Control of Your Time and Your Life.* New York: Peter H. Wyden, Inc., 1973.

SCOTT, D. *How to Put More Time in Your Life.* New York: Rawson, Wade Publishers, Inc., 1980.

WINSTON, S. *Getting Organized: The Easy Way to Bring Order into Your Life.* New York: W. W. Norton & Co., Inc., 1978.

index

Acetaminophen, 60
Acute stress, 30–32
Adrenaline, 31, 32
Aggression:
  assertiveness distinguished from, 92
  See also Passive–aggressive behaviors
Alarm phase, 32, 34
Alternatives, decision making and, 139–40
Amphetamines, 75
Anger (angry feelings), 78–86
  breaking the cycle of, 82–83
  coping with someone else's, 85–86
  cycle leading to the expression of, 79–80
  reactions to, 80–82
  structuring your responses to, 83–85
Antidepressants, 76
Aspirin, 59–60
Assertiveness, 92–96

Assertiveness hierarchy, 93–94
Audio cues, 101–2

Back, massaging your, 107
Backtracking, 157
Bedtime ritual, 50–51
Bedtime snack, 51
Behavioral rehearsal, 104–6
Beverages, 67–68
Biotin, 118
Birth control pills, migraine headaches and, 58–59
Breathing exercises, 99–100
Broken-record technique, 94–95

Caffeine:
  consumption of, 64–66, 113
  in pain relievers, 61
Calcium, 118
Chlorine, 120

Cholesterol, 110, 111
Choline, 118
Clothing, saving money on, 168–69
Cocaine, 77
Codeine, 76–77
Communication, 87–91
    analyzing breakdowns in, 88–89
    preventing breakdowns in, 89–91
Compromises, workable, 95
Confrontation, angry feelings and, 81
Control, perceptions of stress and feeling
    of, 40, 42, 43
Coping behaviors checklist, 7–10
Coping techniques, 97–129
    behavioral rehearsal, 104–6
    breathing exercises, 99–100
    diet, 110–20
    guilty pleasures, 124
    hugs, 128–29
    humor, 127–28
    journals and diaries, 126–27
    meditation, 108–10
    passions (leisure-time activities),
        123–24
    physical fitness, 120–22
    rewards, 124–26
    self-massage, 106–8
    visualization, 100–4
Corticoids, 31, 33, 38
Cousins, Norman, 127
Craziness, as stress response, 38

Death, 38
Decisions (decision making), 138–47
    lifeline and, 141
    mistakes in, 144–47
    risk taking and, 142–44
    wise, 138–40
Denial, 37–38
Depression, 54–56
    antidepressant drugs for, 76
Depression headaches, 57–58
Diaries, keeping, 126–27
Diet(s), 110–20
    migraine headaches and, 57–58
    vitamins and minerals in, 113–20
    weight-loss, 62–63
Disorganized people, 150–54
Diversion, 37

Divide-and-conquer principle, 155, 165
Drinking, 66–68
Drugs, 73–77
    mind-altering, 76–77
    mood-altering, 76
    See also specific drugs

Eating:
    dysfunctional, 61–64
    See also Diet
Effectiveness, 149
Efficiency, 149
Energy level, 33–34
Entertainment, saving money on, 169
Environment, 33
Environment recordings, 102
Exercise, 34
    breathing, 99–100
    fitness and, 121–22
    sleep and, 51
Exhaustion phase, 34

Face massages, 107–8
Fatigue, 53–54
Fiber, dietary, 112
Fitness, physical, 120–22
Fogging, 95
Folacin, 118
Food expenses, 168
Foods:
    processed, 110–12
    See also Diet
Foot massage, 108
Free information, providing, 96
Furniture, saving money on, 169

General Adaptation Syndrome (GAS), 32,
    34, 46
Goals, 136–38
Grief, depression associated with, 55, 56
Guilty pleasures, 124

Head, massaging your, 106
Headaches, 56–61
    depression, 57–58
    migraine, 58–59
    tension, 57, 59–60
Heredity, 32–33
Hugs, 128–29
Humor, 127–28

Illness:
  psychosomatic, *see* Psychosomatic illnesses
  as stress response, 38
Information:
  decision-making mistakes and, 144–47
  providing free, 96
Insomnia, 48–52
Interruptions, dealing with, 161–63
Iron, 119

"Job jar" technique, 165–66
Journals, keeping, 126–27

Leisure-time activities, 123–24
Life experiences checklist, 18–22
Lifeline, 140–41
Life satisfaction checklist, 12–18
Listening, 91, 146–47

Magnesium, 119
Margarine, 111
Marijuana, 77
Massage, self-, 106–8
Meats, 111
Meditation, 108–10
Migraine headaches, 58–59
Milk and milk products, 51, 113
Mind-altering drugs, 76–77
Minerals, 113–16, 118–20
Money, management of, 166–70
Mood-altering drugs, 76
Morphine, 76–77

Narcolepsy, 53
Neck massage, 106–7
Negative assertion, 95–96
Negative inquiry, 96
Negotiation, angry feelings and, 81
"No contact" times, 161–62
Noradrenaline, 31, 32

Obligations, risk taking and, 143, 144
Oils, 111
Organization, 148–57
  divide-and-conquer principle of, 155
  underlying principles of, 153–54
  See also Time
Organization game plan, 154–55
Overeating, 61–63
Overweight, 63–64

Pain relivers, 59–61
Panic, 81
Pantothenic acid, 118
Passions (leisure-time activities), 123–24
Passive–aggressive behaviors, 81
Perception Quotient, 42–44
Perceptions of stress, 39–44
Personality type checklist, 22–29
Personality types (or styles), perceptions of stress and, 41
Phosphorus, 118–19
Physical activity, 121–22
  See also Exercise
Physical fitness, 120–22
Physicians, 46–48
Potassium, 120
Power analysis, 80, 83
Procrastination, 164–66
Psychoacoustics, 101–2
Psychosomatic illnesses (or problems), 38, 45–48
  checking out symptoms of, 46–48
  General Adaptation Syndrome and, 46
  psychoanalytic theory of, 45–46

Resistance phase, 32, 34
Resources:
  perception of stress and, 39–40, 42, 43
  risk taking and, 143
Responsibilities, risk taking and, 143, 144
Rewards, 124–26
Rights as a human being, 92–94
Risks, taking, 142–44

Salt, 110, 112, 120
Satir, Virginia, 128
Schneider, John, 19
Self-disclosure, 96
Self-esteem, risk taking and, 142, 144
Self-massage, 106–8
Selye, Hans, 30–32, 34
Sensate focusing, 70–72
Sex, 68–72
Shoulders, massaging your, 107
Sleep:
  hours of, 48–49
  prime time for, 49–50
  scheduling your, 50
  See also Insomnia
Sleep apnea, 53–54

Sleeping pills, 51–52
Smoking, 66–67
Snacks, bedtime, 51
Sodium, 120
Spending plan, personal, 166–68
Stress:
    acute, 30–32
    chronic, 31–32
    perceptions of, 39–44
    physiological side of, 30–34
    reactions to, 37–38
    See also specific topics
Stress patterns, 35–37
Stress symptom checklist, 10–12
Sugar, 110, 112
Support systems, risk taking and, 142–44
Syntonic Research, Inc., 102

Tension headaches, 57, 59–60
Time:
    managing, 157–61
    saving, 163–64
    See also Interruptions, dealing with;
    Procrastination
"To Do" list, 159–61
Tolerance, 37
Trace elements, 119
Track record, perception of stress and, 40,
    42, 43

Trade-offs, time management and, 159
Tranquilizers, 73–74
Transportation, saving money on, 169
Type A personality, 22, 28, 29
Type B personality, 22, 28
Type C personality, 22, 28–29

Values, 130–36
    checking out your, 134–35
    perception of stress and, 39, 41–43
Values clarification, 131–32
Values grid, 134–35
Van der Rohe, Mies, 153–54
Vegetables, 111
Visualization, 100–4
Vitamin/mineral supplements, 113–20
Vitamins, 113–18

Walking, 122
Weight, 62–64
Weight-loss diets, 62–63
Wish lists, 136–37
Withdrawal, 37
    anger and, 80

Zinc, 119